ENRICHING EARLY MATHEMATICAL LEARNING

ENRICHING EARLY MATHEMATICAL LEARNING

Grace Cook, Lesley Jones,
Cathy Murphy and
Gillian Thumpston

OPEN UNIVERSITY PRESS
Buckingham · Philadelphia

Open University Press
Celtic Court
22 Ballmoor
Buckingham
MK18 1XW

and
1900 Frost Road, Suite 101
Bristol, PA 19007, USA

First Published 1997

A catalogue record of this book is available from the British Library

ISBN 0 335 19666 7 (pbk)

Library of Congress Cataloging-in-Publication Data

Enriching early mathematical learning/Grace Cook . . . (et al.).
     p.   cm.
  Includes bibliographical references (p.   –   ) and index.
  ISBN 0-335-19666-7 (pbk.)
  1. Mathematics—Study and teaching (Primary)   I. Cook, Grace.
  1947–
  QA135.5.E56   1997
  372.7′044—dc20   96–43623
                                                        CIP

Typeset by Type Study, Scarborough
Printed in Great Britain by St Edmundsbury Press,
Bury St Edmunds, Suffolk

Contents

Introduction

The basic philosophy which underlies this book is that mathematics is far more than a body of knowledge. It can be seen as a participant process; one in which children can become actively and creatively involved. Children should be given the opportunity in mathematics to make decisions, to formulate and explore their own problems and to communicate their ideas.

Enriching Early Mathematical Learning is written for teachers of children aged five to seven (Key Stage 1) who are trying to enhance their mathematical provision for the children they teach. It gives practical guidance that has a firm theoretical grounding. The ideas included in the book have been developed as a direct result of our experiences in the classroom, in initial teacher education and in running INSET courses.

One of the purposes of this book is to support teachers to work in an open-ended way. We acknowledge that this can be difficult for a teacher who feels less than confident with his or her own mathematical ability. We have tried to address this within the structure we have laid out for each activity.

Each activity contains a starting point and three other pages supporting the implementation of this starting point.

- The *starting point* page includes details about the kind of experiences children will need to have had prior to the activity, the resources needed, the language focus, the next stages of progression and an indication of how it fits into the curriculum. The last indicates both how the work might link with class topics and how it fits into the National Curriculum Programmes of Study.
- *Setting the scene* contains guidance about the organisation of the activity, additional detail about the way in which the activity fits into the programme of study and suggestions about ways in which the activity can help you to assess the children's understanding.
- *What might happen* suggests ways in which children may react and provides some advice about the way teachers might provide immediate support for the child in the context of the activity.
- *Supporting children's learning* suggests ways in which teachers can use the assessments they have made to plan appropriately for the children according to their needs.

Teaching and learning mathematics

Making human sense

This book is intended to help teachers of children in the early years to plan mathematical experiences which are rich in potential. It is designed to give easy access to ideas, but also to support teachers as they plan for progression throughout the ability levels. The focus is on the use and application of mathematics, reflecting the view that children learn by constructing their own knowledge (Cobb 1986; Lerman 1989; Skemp 1989) and that skills learnt in isolation are not necessarily transferred to relevant applications. Children need to use and apply their mathematical skills and knowledge in meaningful situations in order to develop their understanding. In *Children's Minds* (1978), Margaret Donaldson challenges some of Piaget's findings and demonstrates how introducing human sense into a situation enables children to succeed at tasks they could not manage in the abstract. Martin Hughes (1986) worked with Donaldson and his work emphasizes that children need to see a reason for using and learning mathematics. In one piece of research he worked with a group of children who were regularly using '+ and –' symbols in the classroom situation, but who had not internalised their use and did not use them in a different context. By involving the children in games in which they needed to use symbols, he sought to develop the children's understanding of the need for symbols. He recommends that teachers should be 'as explicit as possible in explaining to children what the symbols are called, what they look like and why they are used' (p. 178).

Building on previous experiences

As a result of experiences in exploring and making sense of their world, children first come to school bringing with them a wealth of understanding. This occurs in a holistic way, not separated into different subject strands. Their experience in school should build on this by providing practical situations where children have time to play, explore, experiment and consolidate their earlier learning. How children construct their learning varies from child to child. For example, some children develop mental imagery which provides a visual model for mathematics, while others appear to rely more on symbolic representation. Since mathematics is essentially an abstract subject, it is necessary to provide a variety of practical experiences which scaffold the children's learning (Vygotsky 1978) and enable them to extract common concepts. It is therefore essential for teachers to be able to use a wealth of strategies and approaches.

The role of language

Parents and teachers support children in their learning through talking and questioning, and so provide and develop appropriate language. The teacher's role in language development can take different forms:

- running commentary;
- questioning;
- observing and listening.

By providing a 'running commentary' on the children's activities the teacher can validate and extend their vocabulary (Pound et al. 1992). There will be times when it is appropriate to question the children about their activities. They can be encouraged to predict what might happen and to consider their reasons for decisions they make, e.g. 'How did you work that out?' or 'What made you decide to pour that in there?' Children will vary in their ability to respond to these questions, but by posing the questions, adults will prompt them to reflect and reason. Often a child is so deeply involved in an exploration that an intervention by the adult might be an intrusion into the child's thinking. Choosing to remain silent is a valid professional decision. Observing children at work, even when they are silent, can provide valuable insights for assessment purposes. Listening to their discussion provides further information about their ability to communicate, but it is important to bear in mind that children's language skills may not be as advanced as their conceptual development. In all of these interactions with young children the teacher's role is most valuable when they take place in an environment of genuine dialogue.

Organising and managing mathematics learning

Creating a supportive environment

In writing this book we have had in mind a classroom in which the children know that their ideas are welcomed and valued. Ideally, teachers will engender an atmosphere in which children regularly listen to each other's views and respect them, even if they are different from their own. This is very much easier to bring about if it forms part of a whole school policy and applies to all areas of the curriculum. An atmosphere of this kind, which may take some time to create, can build children's confidence about offering their views. Once children know that their views will be taken into account they will be encouraged to reflect upon their own thinking and eventually be able to verbalise their thought processes.

Teachers constructing their own knowledge

It is vital for teachers to plan carefully in order to maximise teaching opportunities. However, planning needs to be sufficiently flexible to allow children the opportunity to pursue their own lines of development. We consider it important that the teacher develops his or her own 'mental map' as a framework for the learning that might take place. This personal framework allows the teacher to be able to make a professional judgement about the appropriateness of the child's exploration and will aid further planning. We recognise that this 'mental map' provides a planning framework for the teacher, but is not necessarily mirrored in the child's conceptual development. See Denvir and Brown (1986) for an analysis of children's conceptual development. The notion of a 'mental map' has guided our thinking in the writing of this book. We have tried to identify pathways in mathematics learning which may help teachers to develop their own 'mental map'. We recognise that some of the links we have made are linear in fashion, as indicated by the sections 'What before?' and 'What next?' in each activity. Others form a more comprehensive network, indicated by cross-referencing between activities in the book and the National Curriculum Programmes of Study. In the process of writing the book we have been surprised at the extent to which the activities link together and reinforce process skills introduced elsewhere. We hope that in working through the activities with children, teachers will make their own connections and so strengthen their own understanding of primary mathematics (constructing their own knowledge).

Presenting activities

One of the techniques which we refer to at various points in the book is 'modelling'. This is no strange and fanciful idea, but one which we believe many teachers use on a regular basis. It is a way of introducing an activity whereby the teacher guides the children into the mathematics, by doing the activity together with the children. The teacher can then draw the children into making suggestions about the way in which the activity might proceed. In this way all the children have access to what is required of them. It should mean that you avoid the 'What have I got to do?' questions and once the activity is under way you should be able to leave the group to continue. This will allow you an opportunity to support and challenge individuals further or to work with another group of children.

Whole class teaching

We consider that time spent with the whole class together in a carpeted area of the classroom (if possible) should form an essential part of teachers' daily planning, both to introduce the activity and for feedback at the end. At this time there is an opportunity for consolidating the learning objectives, sharing mental methods, communicating findings, developing mathematical language and extending mathematical thinking through questions, both teacher's and children's.

The starting points for each of the activities in the book are ones which can arise in any classroom, and they are ideas which have worked for us. Throughout the book there is an emphasis on teachers observing children at work and questioning them about their strategies. We use the term observation to include watching, listening and recording children's talk and actions, and noting what they cannot do as well as their achievements. The findings from this observation can be used to inform future planning. The child's learning experience may occur in a holistic way, but the teacher needs to have a clear idea of a route through mathematics, in order to extend and consolidate the child's learning.

Within this introduction we have talked about *enriching* the curriculum, *challenging* the children and *planning* learning experiences based on *assessment* of children's attainment and understanding. In recent years primary education has undergone a great deal of change and teachers have had to respond to many pressures from outside agencies. In some cases this had led to teachers feeling that they must 'play safe' and work on consolidating 'basic skills' (this term usually refers to computation). We believe that all children are entitled to a rich and challenging curriculum, appropriately planned for them, based on an assessment of their needs. We hope that the book will help to bring this about. It reflects our views of mathematics and the way in which it is learnt by young children. We believe mathematics to be a broad area of knowledge which provides the opportunity for children to be challenged intellectually and to achieve cognitively satisfying experiences. There is an aesthetic side to mathematics which children are entitled to experience, and their entitlement extends to a quality experience in all aspects of the mathematics curriculum. The mathematics which they will meet should be firmly rooted in their early experience, but should allow them the opportunity to extend their experience and develop new ideas. We recognise that most of the activities within the book require the teacher to work intensively with one group of children at a time. We make no apology for this, believing that teachers of children in the early years recognise the need to give quality time to work with individual children on their mathematical skills. We suggest that, just as for reading, quality time should also be given to children, both individually and in groups, to develop their understanding of mathematics.

References

Cobb, P. (1986) Context, goals, beliefs and learning mathematics, *For the Learning of Mathematics*, 6(2), 2–9.

Denvir, B. and Brown, M. (1986) Understanding of number concepts in low attaining 7–9 year olds, *Educational Studies in Mathematics*, 17, 15–36 and 143–64.

Donaldson, M. (1978) *Children's Minds*. London: Fontana.

Hughes, M. (1986) *Children and Number*. Oxford: Basil Blackwell.

Lerman, S. (1989) Investigations: where to now?, in P. Ernest (ed.) *Mathematics Teaching: The State of the Art*. Lewes: Falmer.

Pound, L., Cook, L., Court, J., Stevenson, J. and Wadsworth, J. (1992) *The Early Years: Mathematics*. London: Harcourt, Brace, Jovanovich.

Skemp, R.R. (1989) *Mathematics in the Primary School*. London: Routledge.

Vygotsky, L.S. (1978) *Mind in Society: the Development of the Higher Psychological Processes*. London: Harvard University Press.

Activities linked to the National Curriculum Programmes of Study

	Using and applying				Number					Shape, space and measures			
	1	2	3	4	1	2	3	4	5	1	2	3	4
Handfuls	✔		✔	✔	✔	✔				✔			✔
Ladybirds	✔		✔	✔	✔	✔	✔						
Rosie the hen	✔		✔	✔	✔	✔	✔						
Jumps and hops	✔		✔	✔	✔		✔						
Number ladder	✔		✔	✔	✔		✔						
Calculator numbers	✔	✔			✔	✔	✔						
Higher and lower	✔		✔		✔	✔							
Secret number	✔	✔	✔	✔	✔		✔						
Feely bag pairs	✔		✔						✔	✔	✔		
Boxes	✔	✔	✔	✔						✔	✔		✔
Comparing containers	✔		✔	✔									✔
Towers	✔	✔	✔	✔						✔	✔		✔
Robots	✔	✔	✔	✔	✔	✔				✔		✔	✔
Wrapping paper	✔	✔	✔	✔						✔	✔	✔	
Here comes the dustcart	✔		✔	✔	✔				✔				
Dolly mixtures	✔		✔	✔	✔					✔	✔	✔	
Fabric beanies	✔		✔	✔	✔					✔	✔		✔
What's missing?	✔	✔	✔	✔	✔	✔	✔			✔	✔	✔	
Egg boxes	✔	✔	✔	✔						✔		✔	
Unifix towers	✔	✔			✔	✔	✔		✔				

HANDFULS

What before?

Some experience of counting.

Resources

Pairs of paper hands (different colours for each child) and one pair for the teacher.

Baskets with objects of a reasonable size, i.e. not too small.

Handfuls

Give yourself and the children a pair of paper hands to act as workspaces.

Select one of the baskets of objects and pick some up with one of your hands. Put the objects on the appropriate paper hand. Count, with the children, how many you have picked up. Ask the children to predict how many objects you will pick up with your other hand and to give reasons for their predictions.

Pick up the second handful of objects, put them on the other paper hand and count them together. Ask,'Did one hand hold more than the other?' and match 1:1 to check.

Each child then takes his or her own handful from the first basket of objects, taking care to put each handful on a different paper hand. 'How many did you pick up in each hand?'

Can they find out which hand held more/fewer?

Each child could then go on to repeat the activity with the similar sized objects in the other baskets.

Language

Right, left.

How many, more, fewer, the same.

Number names.

How it fits

With topics

Part of a topic on ourselves.
Part of a topic on capacity.
Part of a topic on senses.

With National Curriculum

- Developing mathematical language and communication.
- Developing mathematical reasoning.
- Developing an understanding of place value.
- Understanding and using measures.

What next?

Different objects in the baskets.

Smaller objects, e.g. pegs, pennies, small buttons.

What if you wear gloves to pick things up? Mittens?

Make an interactive display for ongoing, independent activity.

HANDFULS

Setting the scene

You will need to work with the group and watch carefully while they are doing this activity. Your modelling of the activity with the children's involvement provides a way in for all of the children and gives you a chance to make an initial assessment of each child's counting ability and how they might set about comparing the number of members of a set.

(As discussed in the Introduction, your modelling of this activity *could* be demonstrated to the whole class in order that groups could work independently and share their findings.)

Developing mathematical language and communication

By listening to children's responses to the question, 'Did one hand hold more/fewer than the other?' you can determine their level of understanding of this specific mathematical language concerned with number.

By watching when the children themselves are taking handfuls you can observe their understanding of comparison.

Developing mathematical reasoning

This activity allows the children to predict how many objects will be picked up after they have counted your initial handful and to explain their prediction. This can be reinforced as they continue with the activity. It is important to continue to ask them to make predictions and to explain them. This will encourage them to develop their reasoning and make decisions based on prior knowledge and experience. It will also allow you to determine whether these predictions are sensible and becoming more precise. Valuing the children's explanations even if they are bizarre helps the children to begin to realise that their thinking process is important to you.

Developing an understanding of place value

The main focus of this activity is to develop children's abilities to count and compare collections of objects and to find a way of checking their comparison (ordering). One of the ways of comparing sets is to match 1:1, arranging the two sets in pairs so that they can be matched.

This allows the children to see which set has more and which fewer and is an early stage of looking at 'difference' as an aspect of subtraction.

Understanding and using measures

Through children explaining their predictions you will be able to determine the extent to which they understand the general notion of 'the smaller the unit (object) the more I can pick up (capacity)'.

HANDFULS

What might happen

If you are using objects which are already familiar to the children in the classroom you will find that the children focus quickly on the activity.

When the group are counting your initial handful you may notice that a child cannot say the number names. In this case you may decide to let the child continue to hear the number names repeated by yourself and other children.

Children may predict unreasonably or may not be prepared to predict at all, even though you have counted the original handful. Hearing the other children's predictions and explanations will help. It is important to accept the children's lack of confidence/understanding in order to encourage them to feel positive about predicting in the future. Make a note of this to be followed up later.

When you ask, 'Did one hand hold more than the other?' some children will count each set and will know that one set has more than the other. It is still useful for those children to see you matching 1:1 to check, in order to reinforce the concept of order. Matching 1:1 will also support the children who do not have a concept of 'more'.

When the children are counting their own handfuls they may not count accurately. You may have to help them by counting with them and moving each object as you do so. Continue to ask the children questions such as 'Which hand holds more/fewer?', 'How can you find out?', 'How many do you think you will pick up this time?'

Some children will be able to explain their comparison clearly and confidently. You may wish to offer them the opportunity to use smaller objects, challenging them to count larger numbers.

Links with other activities in this book:

Calculator numbers (page 26)   Number ladder (page 22)
Ladybirds (page 10)   Higher and lower (page 30)
Secret number (page 34)

Supporting children's learning

Children who cannot say the number names

Involve the children in number rhymes and songs. Use number as a part of classroom organisation, e.g. counting the children in the class, around the table, on the carpet, in the home corner. At carpet-time talk about birthdays, age etc. In fact, exploit every opportunity to count with the children.

HANDFULS

Children who have difficulty with predicting

You need to create a supportive environment in which all children feel confident enough to take risks. This means initially accepting both wrong and right answers, followed by sensitive questioning of how they obtained their answers, which may lead them to recognise the right answer.

Over time the child who lacks confidence in predicting should be supported by this strategy but she or he may also need many opportunities to extend her or his experience of counting sets of objects. Children could also be given the responsibility of making sets for other children to estimate before being asked to estimate themselves.

Similarly, children who make wild guesses need further experience of counting objects. The children can contribute to making a class estimating table, e.g. 'How many sweets in the jar?' 'How many pieces of Lego have been used to make this model?'

Children who are unable to work out which set has more

These children need more experience of comparing unequal sets where the process requires them to match the two sets, e.g. 'Are there enough pencils for each child at the table to have one?' 'Can you check if all the cups are tidied in the home corner by matching to the hooks on the dresser?'

As these activities may not develop the language of more and fewer, it will be necessary to introduce a range of more structured activities where you can intervene or model the process and the language. Introduce games which require each of two players to collect a set of objects, e.g. butterflies on a flower, and also require them to compare their sets to determine who has won.

Children who are unable to count accurately

When children are first counting they often do not know where they have started and so where to end. Very young children may count up to the last number name they know, no matter what size the set is. They need to learn to match each number name to each object. They can be helped to do this by physically moving each object as they say the number name. It is essential that they use objects rather than pictures on a page so that the objects can be moved. In a game, instead of a die, beans which are painted on one side can be cast. The child can count the number which land coloured side up by moving them as they count.

Extensions

Smaller objects could be used so that children are required to count larger numbers. This may lead to grouping in tens and the beginnings of place value. Some challenges could be 'Can you pick up exactly 30 pegs?' or 'Count one handful of butter beans. How many handfuls of butter beans will it take to fill this plant pot? Estimate the number of beans in the pot.'

Ask the children to find a way of recording their findings for the initial handfuls activity, either on the paper hands you have given them or in any other way they feel is appropriate.

LADYBIRDS

What before?

Some experience of counting.

Matching 1:1.

Conservation.

Resources

'Ladybirds': broad beans or counters.

'Leaves' made of green material.

Ladybirds

Give each child, and yourself, a 'leaf'. Put about six 'ladybirds' on top of your leaf and ask the children to put the same number of 'ladybirds' on top of their 'leaves'. Make sure all the children agree that you all have the same number. Put some of your 'ladybirds' under your leaf. Can the children say how many are under the leaf? Tell each child, in turn, to secretly put some of his or her 'ladybirds' under his or her 'leaf'. Ask the rest of the group each time to work out how many are under the 'leaf' and to explain how they did it.

Ask 'Can you each have a different number of "ladybirds" under your leaf?'

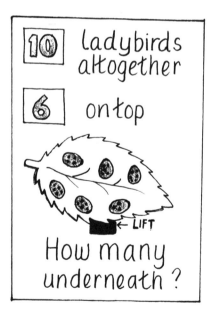

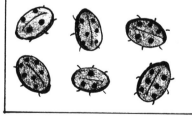

Language

Under, on top.

Number names (one to ten).

How many, more, fewer, the same.

How it fits

With topics

Part of a topic on minibeasts.

With National Curriculum

- Developing mathematical language and communication.
- Developing mathematical reasoning.
- Developing an understanding of place value.
- Understanding relationships between numbers and developing methods of computation.

What next?

More ladybirds.

Can you find *all* the different ways the ladybirds can be spread on top and under the leaf?

Make a story book.

LADYBIRDS

Setting the scene

This small group activity is teacher-intensive. You may decide to spend short spells (5–10 minutes) with the group at one time, leaving them to continue exploring the materials while you work with other groups. Depending on the previous experience and ability of the group, you may be able to spend longer with them. Children who have not fully gained the concept of conservation can engage with this activity but may not be able to benefit from the full extent of the activity.

You will need to consider the organisation and management of this task. If you add Velcro to the back of each ladybird they are less likely to escape from the leaves!

It is useful to have a notebook with you to jot down what you notice about each child and his or her approach to the task. These brief notes will help you with assessment and allow you to develop the task from the children's responses.

Developing mathematical language and communication

By listening to the children and observing their responses you will be able to determine how well their understanding of the language of number has developed. Do they know what six is? When you ask them to put the same number of ladybirds on their leaf do they understand that concept?

Instructing the children to put ladybirds 'on top of' and 'under' their leaves is also important for developing positional language.

Developing mathematical reasoning

By asking the children to say how many ladybirds have been put under the leaf when they can only see the ones that are on top, you are encouraging them to 'picture' the objects in their heads and to 'see' the relationship between those ladybirds that are visible and the total number that you had to begin with. This is a difficult concept for young children but allowing them to predict and then find out about their prediction, using relatively small numbers, can help them to develop this abstraction.

Developing an understanding of place value

This activity requires the children to count up to six, and to appreciate that this number remains the same unless some ladybirds are added to the set, or taken away. This conservation of number is of crucial importance in an understanding of the abstract concept of number. It creates a firm foundation on which to build operations such as addition and subtraction.

Understanding relationships between numbers and developing methods of computation

Children are exploring patterns in addition and subtraction and may begin to recognise the relationship between these two operations by manipulating the ladybirds both physically and mentally. Again, the use of a relatively small number of ladybirds facilitates this. The children can begin to really get to know the number six and how it can be made by other smaller numbers.

LADYBIRDS

What might happen

The children may want to play with the ladybirds and the leaves and talk about them, but this is not an integral part of this activity.

You may have to support some of the children in taking the correct number of ladybirds. This support may be given by making a statement such as 'Let's see if we've all got the same number on our leaves.' Follow this by counting together how many ladybirds each child has got. The children who do have difficulties with counting correctly may find the rest of the activity very demanding, but with support can persevere.

A child who has been able to count accurately may still always have to look under the leaf before confirming the number of ladybirds that are hidden. This may be because she or he cannot visualise the number or because she or he does not have a firm idea of the conservation of number. The children are being asked to think algebraically in this activity. They need to hold the total number of ladybirds in their heads in order to calculate the number 'underneath'.

At the beginning of the activity some children may need to look under the leaf to confirm the number of ladybirds, but as they become more confident and more aware of the pattern they are able to predict. A question such as 'How did you know how many were underneath?' should be asked whenever a child has predicted either correctly or incorrectly. If children cannot verbalise what they have done 'in their heads' this can be followed up at a later time.

Some children will be able to calculate the number of 'missing' ladybirds in their heads. Questioning them as above will encourage them to clarify and articulate their thinking and may help the other children in the group.

Links with other activities in this book:

Rosie the hen (page 14)   Secret number (page 34)

LADYBIRDS

Supporting children's learning

Children who cannot take the correct number of ladybirds

These children may need further experiences of counting, one-to-one correspondence and conservation activities. These may be experienced in a variety of situations, including everyday classroom activities such as giving out pencils, laying the table for a set number of children or number rhymes. More formal activities should also be used, e.g.

> What different models can be made with six lego pieces? Make a table display for other children to add to.

A child who is able to count but not able to calculate the number of missing ladybirds

More experience of activities which are very similar might be needed, e.g.

> Take a lace with five cubes on it. 'I'm going to hang it over the edge of the table so that you can only see some of the cubes. How many are hanging down?'

> Take six beans. Hide some under a yogurt pot and put some on top. 'How many are hidden?'

> Try hiding all six ladybirds under the leaf first and bringing some to the top.

Helping children to visualise numbers

Ask the children to 'picture' numbers in their head. 'Close your eyes. When I say "five" what do you see in your head? Can you tell me what you see? Can you draw what you see? Imagine five cats, six pennies.' Instruct the children to rearrange their images: put the pennies in a long line, put them like the dots on a die etc. The children may need to see the six pennies first before picturing them in their heads.

Helping children to verbalise what they see

The children can be given 'picturing' instructions, e.g. 'put six pennies into two groups; into two groups in a different way; into three groups.' These instructions may generate different images for each of the children. After the separate visualisations, each child is required to describe what he or she saw, perhaps drawing at the same time. If the children wish to draw without speaking you could offer the descriptive language for them. By hearing your description and those of their friends these children will be supported in developing both the appropriate language and the confidence to speak.

Extensions

Repeat the activity with larger numbers and in different contexts.

Ask the children to check and justify that they have found all the possible ways to arrange the ladybirds.

Make a story book showing the arrangements (see Appendix).

ROSIE THE HEN

What before?

Some experience of counting.

Comparing sets of five objects.

One-to-one correspondence.

Resources

Rosie the hen made from card or fabric. She needs 'working' wings with a Velcro strip under each wing and a set of five chicks. (See Appendix.)

Rosie the hen

You need one hen, constructed from fabric or card, and a set of five chicks.

Ask the children to count the chicks out loud. Make sure all the children are sure that there are five chicks altogether.

Turn so that Rosie is out of sight. Place three chicks under one wing and two under the other.

Show the children the chicks under one wing and ask how many chicks are under the other wing.

Let the children take turns to hide some chicks under one wing and the rest under the other, so that all five chicks are used each time.

The child who has hidden the chicks shows the chicks under one wing and asks how many are under the other wing.

Language

Counting, visualising.

Number names.

One-to-one correspondence.

Cardinal number, reasoning.

How it fits

With topics

Part of a topic on animals.
Part of a topic on farms.
Part of a topic on trails.
Link with the story 'Rosie's Walk'.

With National Curriculum

- Developing mathematical language and communication.
- Developing mathematical reasoning.
- Developing an understanding of place value, leading to an understanding of relationships between numbers and the development of methods of computation.

What next?

Different numbers of chicks.

Children record their work.

ROSIE THE HEN

Setting the scene

This activity is teacher-led and very much focused on discussion, helping the children to develop skills of visualising and manipulating numbers and to verbalise what they are thinking?

Initially you will need to work with a small group or with all of the children when they are gathered together (e.g. on a carpeted area). The children may want to talk about the hen. Allowing them some time for this will enable them to focus on the mathematics. You need to place some emphasis on the idea that all the chicks are used each time the game is played. Rosie can then be left for children to play with and explore on their own. *Note:* To challenge the children you might change the number of chicks each day.

Developing mathematical language and communication

As the children take turns, they can be encouraged to ask questions which are clearly phrased. When you initially model the situation you can ask different questions:

'Are there any chicks under the other wing?' 'How do you know that?'

'How many chicks are under the other wing?' 'How do you know that?'

'Are there more chicks under the other wing?'

'Are there fewer chicks under the other wing?'

By listening to the questions children ask and to the language they use you can assess their level of understanding of specific mathematical vocabulary and their ability to communicate in mathematics. Asking the children how they know the answer may help you to access their method of reasoning.

Developing mathematical reasoning

Children need to begin to think algebraically, with an awareness of the whole number and its constituent parts. This is particularly challenging when you introduce the number zero. There is also an element of logical thinking embedded in this task. It might be helpful to introduce 'if . . . then . . .' statements. 'If there are no chicks under this wing, then there must be five chicks under the other wing.'

Developing an understanding of place value leading to an understanding of the relationships between numbers and the development of methods of computation

In order to answer the questions correctly the children need to have a good understanding of the cardinal aspect of the number and of conservation of number. They will frequently be counting and checking the total number of chicks. It can provide an early opportunity for children to explore patterns in addition and subtraction.

ROSIE THE HEN

What might happen

As this is a focused discussion activity it is almost impossible to cover all the responses that children might make to a particular situation. If a child seems to respond in a way that you do not understand, try to find out why. You will need to create an atmosphere in which children know that you value them thinking carefully about their responses. As children observe their peers explaining their reasoning, they will gradually understand that they need to think carefully about their answers.

Some children seem to be able to count up to five and to understand that there are only five chicks. However, when you put two chicks under one wing and three under the other and show them just the chicks under one wing:

1 They look at the chicks under one wing and say there are five. This may be because the child has attached a number name to each chick instead of to the whole set, and in her eyes 'number five' is still there even though there may be a smaller set.
2 They make wild guesses and have no apparent reason for the guesses. This may be because young children like to give an answer to a question even if they do not know.
3 They count the chicks they can see and say that there are the same number under the other wing. This may also be because they like to give an answer to a question, but if they have counted three under one wing it may seem sensible to guess that there are three under the other.
4 They count the chicks they can see but will not 'guess' how many there are under the other wing. This may be because the children do not want to give an incorrect answer. They may realise that there should be five chicks but as they can see only three and cannot yet 'picture' how many are under the other wing they will not guess.

With all of these responses support the children by looking under each wing, counting how many chicks are there, and ascertaining that there are still five altogether.

Some children will confidently predict how many chicks are under the 'other' wing but will not be able to explain how they know. Hearing other children's explanations will help children to develop this skill.

Links with other activities in this book:

Handfuls (page 6)   Secret number (page 34)
Ladybirds (page 10)

16

ROSIE THE HEN

Supporting children's learning

There are three main areas with which children may need support in this activity: visualising, verbalising and manipulating numbers. Children may need support in more than one of these areas. Most of this support will take place during the activity.

Children can be helped to progress during the discussion which takes place in this activity.

Children who have mentally given each chick a number name

These children have not yet understood the cardinal aspect of number, i.e. that the last number name labels the set. Such children need plenty of counting experiences, e.g. 'How many children sitting at the table?' 'How many pencils in the pot?' 'How many do we need for each child to have a pencil?' 'How many children are lining up at the door?' In each case the set can be changed around and recounted in any order, to emphasise that the size of the set remains the same.

Children who make wild guesses, and children who guess the same number as the chicks under the first wing

Such children need help with visualising the original number. Giving a context to the problem, by setting it in a story, will help them to focus clearly on the original number, e.g. 'Rosie has all five of her chicks under this wing, but they are very squashed. Some of them have wriggled out and gone under the other wing. Can we work out how many have gone?'

To provide additional support for children to hold the original number, you could start the story from the time when the chicks hatched. Provide an egg to match each chick and leave all the eggs in sight as the chicks disappear under the wings. The children can then use one-to-one correspondence to help them to calculate how many chicks are missing.

Additional help for children who need to visualise the situation

Children will be helped to visualise the situation if they are more familiar with the ways in which sets can be partitioned, e.g. a set of six biscuits arranged on two plates. How many different ways can they be arranged? (see Baratta-Lorton 1979; Bird 1991).

Children should be encouraged to do some mental mathematics. For example, imagine six counters. Arrange them in a row, then move them into two rows. How many will there be in each row?

Children who can confidently predict how many chicks there are, but cannot explain their thinking

By modelling this you can help children to 'get inside their own heads' to find an explanation of their reasoning. In order to do this, children need to reflect on their reasoning and to find the language necessary to express this.

Extensions

Different numbers of chicks might be used. Can the children find and check all possible arrangements of the chicks. Ask the children to record their findings, then to explain their written record to others in the class.

JUMPS AND HOPS

What before?

Experience of: different ways of jumping, hopping, skipping.

Counting.

Pattern recognition.

Resources

Skipping ropes.

Tambourine.

Language

Forward, back.

Inside, outside.

Over, side, middle, symmetrical, right, left.

Jumps and hops

Take the children into the hall or playground. Ask the children each to make a circle on the ground with a skipping rope.

Ask them to try different ways of jumping into their shape, around the outside of the rope, in and out, sideways and backwards.

Ask the children to make a pattern of jumps, legs apart, together, apart, together . . . hop, hop, jump, jump, hop, hop . . . side to middle, side to middle, side to middle . . .

Note which children are being systematic in their pattern making. Choose these children to demonstrate individually to the class. Ask the rest of the class to describe the pattern being made. Echo the words as the child repeats the pattern, emphasising the rhythm as you do so.

Let the children choose a partner and show their patterns to each other. Can one partner copy the other's pattern? Ask, 'Can you copy your partner's pattern? Can you continue the pattern?' You can challenge the most able children by asking, 'What will happen on every third movement?'

How it fits

With topics

Topic on patterns.
Ourselves.

With National Curriculum

- Developing mathematical language and communication.
- Developing mathematical reasoning.
- Understanding relationships between numbers and developing methods of computation.

What next?

Children recording their ideas.

Using a floor number line.

Developing more complex patterns.

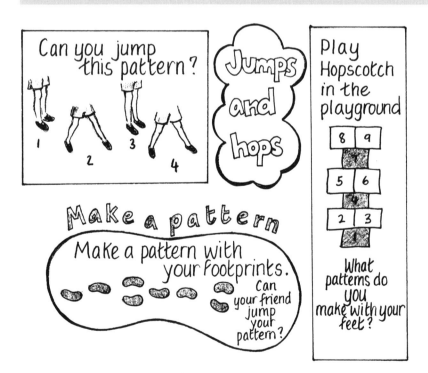

Can you jump this pattern?

1 2 3 4

Jumps and hops

Make a pattern

Make a pattern with your footprints. Can your friend jump your pattern?

Play Hopscotch in the playground

8 9
5 6
2 3

What patterns do you make with your feet?

JUMPS AND HOPS

Setting the scene

The children will need to have experienced some work with pattern prior to this activity. They need to have the notion of a regular pattern as one which repeats itself, e.g. stand, sit, stand, sit, stand, sit. They also need some experience of using their bodies to create a pattern; for instance, with clapping or hopping activities. They will need to know how to continue a pattern and to create their own patterns. This is a whole class activity and can take place in a PE lesson. The tambourine can set a beat on which the children can base their pattern of jumps. The questions you ask will draw the children's attention to the mathematics they are doing. Use any opportunity of children's own variations which could extend the range of mathematics considered. This might include directions, symmetry etc. Draw attention to children's original ideas and discuss them with the class.

Developing mathematical language and communication

This is an unusual medium providing the children with an opportunity to present mathematical ideas through their pattern making. The children will need to discuss in their pairs what the pattern will be, and they will experience making, observing and describing patterns. As they are doing so you will be able to assess their understanding of pattern, by observing their movements and listening to the language they use.

Developing mathematical reasoning

To recognise simple patterns children have to recognise the algebraic relationships which occur. If children are able to say, 'After every jump there is always a hop', this is the first step in *generalising*, which is an essential mathematical activity. Through your questioning they can be encouraged to predict how the pattern will continue and they can check physically.

Understanding relationships between numbers and developing methods of computation

In 'Jumps and hops' children are using repeating patterns to develop their ideas of regularity and sequencing. They will note the regular features of the pattern, e.g. 'The skip always happens on the fourth move.'

JUMPS AND HOPS

What might happen

Some children may have difficulty coordinating their movements sufficiently for this task. Slowing the pace can be helpful. Allowing the children to choose movements which they find less difficult can enable these children to participate.

Some children will not have established a sense of pattern, and compile a string of actions rather than a repeating pattern. Draw their attention to simple patterns produced by other children and encourage the children to say what they see. Ask all the children to copy the pattern they have just watched. You may wish to 'conduct' the rhythm of the pattern yourself by clapping or using an instrument.

Some children may produce a pattern which appears to have no system. Ask the children to explain what they have done in order to ascertain whether or not they have created a repeating pattern.

Some children may begin to produce a pattern, but do not sustain the repetition. Ask them to describe their pattern to you and repeat it back to them, emphasising where the pattern has broken down.

Children who successfully create a pattern can be asked to demonstrate this to the other children and if possible to describe their pattern. There may be some children who cannot describe what the pattern is even though they have demonstrated it.

Children who are confident with this activity might create more adventurous patterns, and careful questioning might extend their thinking by asking them to predict further ahead in the pattern.

Links with other activities in this book:

Wrapping paper (page 58)

JUMPS AND HOPS

Supporting children's learning

Children who have not established a sense of pattern or have no apparent system

Those children who demonstrate little sense of pattern will need extensive practice in making repeating patterns. It is important to include activities which give them a *physical* experience of pattern, such as clapping, marching, standing and sitting in a rhythm. This might take place within a music activity, a PE context or on the carpet. You can also make patterns with the children themselves: boy, boy, girl, boy, boy, girl; or cardigan, sweatshirt, cardigan, sweatshirt. Further experience can be given with a variety of materials, e.g. printing with potatoes, shapes, sponges, hands, making patterns on pegboards, threading beads, block play.

Children who can demonstrate a pattern but cannot describe it, and children who make a pattern but do not sustain it

It may be helpful to work with these children by asking them to make a pattern following your instructions. Encourage them to chant your pattern first. Many of the activities and materials described in the section above would be appropriate for this. While they are making the pattern you can use the opportunity to ask questions which will help them to reflect on their thinking. 'How do you know what comes next?' 'How did you know that you needed more girls?' 'What will come next?' 'How did you work that out?' This will encourage the children to use appropriate mathematical language. When they have completed their repeating pattern ask them to chant through the whole pattern.

Extensions

Where children are able to create patterns and describe them successfully, they can be asked to think of a pattern which they can 'put down on paper' in order to develop it in the next lesson. By establishing a need for the children to find a way of remembering what they have done, you provide a purpose for recording. This visual record can be used in the next lesson. Can other children follow the 'instructions' to recreate the pattern? If not, can the group refine the original record to make it clearer.

Ask the children to try out hopping and jumping patterns along a floor number line. Can they predict where they will land on the next hop, and the next, and the next? What about the jumps? What will it be on number 10? What sort of sequence would give you the five times table?

Sit the class in a circle. Establish a pattern such as clap, pop, click, where each child has a sound to make. Ask the children, 'Will you always make the same sound? Can you predict which sound you will make?' Ask the children to pause, then *you* choose a child who is about ten further on round the circle and ask, 'Which sound will Harriet make? What about Sanjay? How did you know that? How did you work that out?'

As the children become more confident and competent you can make the patterns more complex. Clapping patterns and movement patterns can be developed each day when the class is gathered on the carpet. In activities using a variety of materials, offer the children more adventurous patterns for them to identify and then continue. Encourage them to make more complex patterns themselves.

NUMBER LADDER

What before?

Board games.

Experience of counting steps in PE and outdoor play.

Experience of using unnumbered lines, e.g. coloured footprints.

Whole class discussions with a wall number line.

Resources

Masking tape number ladder or stepping stones across a river, on the classroom floor, marked to 15.

Large soft die or die with numerals.

Language

Number names.

More and fewer.

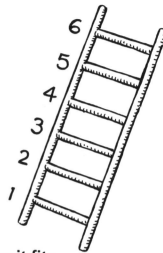

Number ladder

With the class, demonstrate throwing the die and stepping along the number ladder, emphasising counting the steps from 'below' the ladder. Keep throwing the die until you reach the top.

While you are throwing the die and stepping along the ladder ask the children questions such as 'Where do you think I will land this time? How do you know? What number do I need to reach the top of the ladder?' Choose a couple of children to have a turn, re-emphasising the stepping on and asking 'How many more steps do you need to catch up with or get past your partner?' How many throws of the die did you need to get to the top?'

The children can then be sent off, one pair at a time, to have a go on their own. From time to time you should return to the pair of children to observe what they are doing and to extend their thinking by asking questions such as those above.

How it fits

With topics

Part of a topic about 'Jack and the Beanstalk'.
Part of a topic on 'How we count'.
PE or playground games.

With National Curriculum

- Developing mathematical language and communication.
- Developing mathematical reasoning.
- Developing an understanding of place value leading to understanding relationships between numbers and developing methods of computation.

What next?

Counting backwards.

Counting in equal jumps.

Investigating all possible throws of the die.

How could the children record their work?

Play the frog jumping game

Which frog will be the first to get to the other side?

NUMBER LADDER

Setting the scene

This activity is called number ladder, but could be carried out with stepping stones crossing a river, or a number line. An advantage of the ladder metaphor is that the first step is clearly defined as a step forward, or a step up. With stepping stones, the first step takes the child from the bank to the first stepping stone. A ladder can be made on strong card or a carpet runner. It can then be displayed vertically and laid on the floor for the children to step along.

It is helpful to begin the activity with the whole class, as the skill of counting on needs to be emphasised. By modelling the activity for the children, you can point out the importance of the starting point and the fact that you are counting each of your steps. The children also need to watch you counting on from a number other than zero. The children can then work in pairs with you monitoring their work from time to time. When you are with the pairs, watch carefully as they do the activity. This will give you the opportunity to check the children's skill in stepping along the number ladder and to make an initial assessment of each child's counting on ability and his or her recognition of the number digits or the number of spots on the die (depending on which type of die you choose to use).

Developing mathematical language and communication

It is helpful to ask children questions about the activity, e.g. 'What number do you think you'll land on?' 'How much further along are you than your partner?' 'How many throws do you think you need to reach the finish?' 'How many more do you need to catch up/get past/get to ten/get to the end?'

By listening to the children's responses to the questions you can determine their level of understanding in the specific mathematical language concerned with number. Where children are able to record their progress, you will gain additional information about their understanding of symbolic representation.

Developing mathematical reasoning

This activity allows the children to predict how many throws they might need on subsequent 'goes' after they have completed one game and tallied the number of throws. They may also predict how many more steps are needed to reach a certain point. Children may start to recognise simple patterns and number relationships and use these to aid predictions and to explain them. This will encourage them to develop their reasoning and to make decisions based on prior knowledge and experiences. It will also allow you to determine whether these predictions are sensible and becoming more precise. Valuing the children's explanations, even if they are bizarre, helps the children to begin to realise that their thinking process is important to you.

Developing an understanding of place value, and understanding relationships between numbers and developing methods of computation

The main focus of this activity is to develop children's abilities to count, count on and read numbers to 15, using a ladder or line. This provides one of the methods for children to explore and recognise addition and subtraction patterns. Later multiplication and division patterns can be investigated in the same way.

NUMBER LADDER

What might happen

As you are beginning with the whole class it will be difficult to determine what individual children know in detail. Through your questioning, however, you can get a feel for the children for whom the activity will be appropriate and those who may need more input before they can work on their own.

Some children may not recognise the numerals or dots on the die that you are using. They will of course gain from the whole class activity but they would need much more work on counting objects and number recognition before working with a number ladder. (See Handfuls, page 6.)

Some children may recognise the number on the die but cannot relate the number to the process of counting steps. Again the 'modelling' of the task that you do will help them to begin to appreciate this, but they will need more help.

One or two children may be able to match steps to the number on the first throw of the die but revert to counting from 'where they are' for the next throw, e.g. a child may from the first throw be standing on three. She then throws a four and starts the stepping saying 'one' while still on three. This makes her land on six rather than seven. They also need more support with the skill of counting on. Remind the child that she has said 'One' and not moved one step. Ask the child to redo the move, remembering to take the step as she speaks.

Those children who recognise numerals or dots on the die and have the skill of counting on, on unnumbered lines, are the children who will benefit most from this activity.

If, when the children are working in pairs, you notice that the task seems relatively easy, the questions you ask will help to extend the children's thinking. Encourage them to make predictions about where they will land after throwing the die. Suggest that each pair of children plays the game at least three times – more if you feel they are still concentrating.

Some children may count on and predict easily. You could encourage them to find a way to record what they have done.

Links with other activities in this book:

Handfuls (page 6)   Secret number (page 34)
Ladybirds (page 10)   Higher and lower (page 30)
Calculator numbers (page 26)

NUMBER LADDER

Supporting children's learning

Children who do not recognise the numerals or dots on the die

For children who need support in counting objects, see 'Children who are unable to count accurately' in 'Handfuls' (page 9).

Numeral recognition can be addressed in many ways: classroom displays where the numerals match sets of objects; the date; children's birthdays and birthday cards; labels, e.g. two children can play in the sand, five pencils in this pot. Children learn from each other, so allow the children to play dice games with other children to encourage numeral recognition.

Children who recognise the numbers on the die but cannot relate the number to the process of counting steps

There are different ways children might exhibit this. For example, if four is thrown on the die:

1 They count to four but the counting is unrelated to their movements. Counting steps in PE or outdoor play can be a useful way of focusing children on matching the count to each step.
2 They take four steps which are not matched to the rungs. Give the children the opportunity to use unnumbered footprints or stepping stones laid on the floor. Encourage them to count out loud as they put each foot down on a different stone.

The child who counts 'one' without moving

Introduce a die marked with 0, 1, 2 only. The children will see that 0 and 1 have a different outcome. Use of a numbered ladder will emphasise the 'counting on' aspect.

Extensions

You may want children to record different aspects of the game, e.g. who won, recording the result, tallying the number of throws, the sequence of steps they landed on.

Children can devise their own ways of recording, but you may like to provide some photocopied number ladders to support this.

Start at 15 and count backwards.

Count in equal jumps.

Decide whether the children will jump in twos, threes etc. Each throw of the die will tell them how many of these jumps to take.

Ask the children to predict where they might land. Will they land on the top rung? What would happen if the ladder was a different length?

A challenge might be, 'If your ladder is 20 rungs high, what would be good numbers to "jump in" so that you land exactly on the top rung?'

Investigate all possible throws of a die. With a 15-rung ladder and a 1–6 die there are far too many possibilities for most children. Either limit the height of the ladder to about six rungs or limit the numbers on the die to 4, 5 and 6.

CALCULATOR NUMBERS

What before?

Some experience of recognising numerals (number symbols).

Number names – cardinal and ordinal.

Reading digital displays.

Some time to investigate and use the calculator.

Calculator numbers

Give each child a calculator and make sure they can all see a number line. Allow them some time to explore the calculator and observe what they do.

Ask the children:

Do you know how to make numbers appear in the screen?

Do you know how to clear the screen?

Can you find the numbers you want?

Can you get them to appear in the order you want?

What numbers do you know? Your door number, telephone number, age, bus number?

Can you put in the counting numbers, 0, 1, 2, 3 . . .? What happens to the zero?

What happens when you get to 10? Is there a key for 10? How do you enter 10?

What is the biggest number you know? Can you put that into the calculator? Can you say it? The smallest?

Can you make a pattern? Can you make it count in a pattern?

Resources

Calculators.

Paper, pencils, number grids, number lines (overhead projector calculator if available).

Language

Number names (cardinal and ordinal).

Digit, numeral, larger, smaller, greater, higher, lower, order, more, less.

Calculator display, keys, add, subtract, equals, pattern.

How it fits

With topics

Topic on numbers.
Part of a continuing unit of work on numbers.

With National Curriculum

- Developing mathematical language and communication.
- Developing an understanding of place value.
- Understanding the relationships between numbers and methods of computation.

What next?

Using the constant function.

Investigating which numbers can be made with (e.g.) five matchsticks.

Can you make the calculator count backwards in a pattern?

Use a number line to record the numbers displayed. What happens if two children start at the same number and make patterns, each subtracting a different number. Will they meet? Where? Can you say why?

Ask the children to make their own calculators?

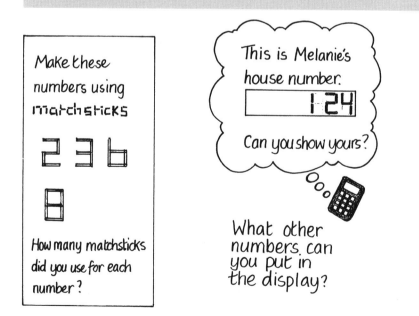

Make these numbers using matchsticks

2 3 6

8

How many matchsticks did you use for each number?

This is Melanie's house number.

1 24

Can you show yours?

What other numbers can you put in the display?

CALCULATOR NUMBERS

Setting the scene

This activity can be started with the whole class, either with each child having a calculator, or with an OHP calculator if you are fortunate enough to have one. If the children have had little experience with calculators they will need time to experiment and see what happens when buttons are pressed. You may need to show the children how to turn them on and off, to explain how calculators work and how to handle them (carefully!). If children are uncomfortable about handling calculators as they see it as 'cheating', it is useful to let the children talk about this and to discuss how the calculator can be used as a tool for finding out, rather than telling them the answer.

When you have asked the initial questions about the numbers that they know, many will want to experiment with other numbers, which will release you to observe your chosen focus group. You may want to bring the class back together several times to discuss the numbers they have generated and to listen to what individual children can do with and have discovered about the calculator.

Developing mathematical language and communication

This activity requires the children to understand and use the language of number.

When you say the number names can the children enter the correct digit into the calculator? Can they read the numerals they have displayed on the screen? Using pencil and paper, can they find a way of showing the numbers they know and/or the ones they have displayed on the screen. By listening to the children's language you will be able to determine the numbers they know and are confident about using.

Developing mathematical reasoning

This activity gives the children an opportunity to use calculators as a means to explore number. They will be using the calculator as a tool to generate numbers and to see what effect the operations and equals keys have on those numbers. This will lead them to make predictions and explain their reasoning. The calculator excites children's interest and enables them to manipulate numbers, an opportunity that other resources may not offer. This experience allows them to be in control, to make decisions and to make sense of the feedback from the machine.

Developing an understanding of place value

The main focus of this activity is to get the children to enter numbers into the calculator and 'read' the numbers in the display. With numbers of more than one digit you may wish to note those children who know in which order they need to press the keys so that they display the chosen number. You will be able to hear which children can recognise and say the number names.

Understanding relationships between numbers and developing methods of computation

When you ask the children to make the calculator count in a pattern it gives them an opportunity to explore number sequences and you will be able to observe their understanding of these. If they are able to make patterns you can ask them to explain what they have done.

CALCULATOR NUMBERS

What might happen

Some children may have difficulty pressing the buttons, pressing either too hard or not hard enough. Encourage the children to leave the calculator on the table to press the keys rather than holding it up to do so.

Children may become completely absorbed with putting numbers into the calculator and forget to say the number names. You may allow this to continue for an appropriate time, but then encourage the children to say which numbers they can see in the display.

Some children may not be able to recognise the numerals or say the number names. You may need to support them by saying the names with them and helping them to find the number on the number line.

Some children are able to read the single digit numbers, and read the larger numbers digit by digit. There are situations in which we read numbers in this way in the adult world, e.g. the 345 bus may be known as the 'three four five'. Echo the children's words, but also use the opportunity to read the number correctly to them: 'three hundred and forty-five'. Make a note for assessment purposes about children's levels of understanding about the number names.

Some children may not initially be able to enter two digit numbers in the correct order. Numbers including zero might prove particularly difficult. The children may self-correct. If not, it may be because their understanding of place value is not fully developed or they have difficulty with left–right orientation. In either case you will want to ask them to read their number and to check if it says what they want it to say. Support them in displaying the number correctly and matching it with the number on the number line.

Some children may choose a number pattern which repeats itself, e.g. {2, 3, 4, 2, 3, 4, 2, 3, 4 . . .} rather than a number sequence. You can ask them which number would come next if there was space in the display. Where would the next 'four' come? This type of pattern may be familiar to children through their work with beads, Unifix, etc.

Some children will be able to make number sequences. You can ask questions like, 'What happens if we keep adding two? Will we ever get to 21? What happens if you start at one instead of zero?'

Some children will have developed confidence and competence with numbers and be able to explain infinity and directed numbers (negative and positive numbers). They will need to be challenged to develop their ideas concerning place value and large numbers, e.g. 'What different numbers can you make using the three digits {2, 6, 7}. Which is the largest number you can make?'

Links with other activities in this book:

Higher and lower (page 30).
Number ladder (page 22)

Secret number (page 34)
Handfuls (page 6)

CALCULATOR NUMBERS

Supporting children's learning

Children who do not read out the numbers and/or cannot say the number names

These children can be given additional practice with reading and saying numbers. You can work with a pack of number cards, holding them up for the children to read and say. This activity can be introduced at a variety of levels, by choosing an appropriate set of cards and using a variety of questions, e.g. 'Whatever card I turn up, I want you to say the number and tell me what one more will be. What about five more, ten more, two fewer, twice as many, half of . . .?' The children can also play this game in pairs. Games with numeral dice and numeral dominoes require children to read and say numbers. The computer program COUNTER (Slimwam 2) provides another way of generating numbers for the children to read. This progam is unusual in that it is one you can use with the whole class on the carpet. If the way in which the numerals are displayed in the calculator presents a difficulty the children can be asked to look carefully at the display. They can then copy the arrangement of the light bars to make the numerals with matchsticks or lolly sticks.

Children who can read single digit numbers and read larger numbers digit by digit, and children who cannot enter two digits in the correct order

Your observation may indicate that the children are ready for place value activities. Introduce activities which involve children in collecting large numbers of cubes etc. (e.g. 'Measure your height in Unifix cubes', 'How many can you hold in your hand?' 'How many does the jar hold?') You can then ask the children to count the cubes. The children can find and read the number on the number line. Place mats marked into sections for tens and units also form a useful resource which can be used together with Dienes MAB, Unifix cubes or everyday objects. The children can then group and exchange the objects, placing number symbols in the sections and reading the number.

Extensions

Let the children explore the constant function. Ask the children to press the following buttons: 2 + = = = etc. (You will need to check exactly how this works on your calculator. On some calculators 2 + + = = gives the constant function.) What do they notice about the numbers that appear in the display? What is the calculator doing? Can you make it count in threes? Starting at 50, can you make the calculator count back in twos to zero? When counting on and back in tens ask the children to focus on the tens column. Can they predict the next number? What is changing each time? What will happen after the nine digit appears in the ten column?

Ask the children to make their own calculator. This could be a physical representation of a calculator using matchsticks for the numbers. It could also be a very large calculator big enough for a child to get inside that could be used as a function machine. One child posts a number in and says what operation the calculator has to do and the child inside displays the correct answer.

The children could also be encouraged to make their own book about calculators with a picture on the front, containing any investigations or discoveries they have made.

HIGHER AND LOWER

What before?

Experience of using calculators.

Some experience of ordering numbers.

Resources

A calculator for each child and one for the teacher.

A butter bean, painted on one side.

Number lines, 0–100, 0–200 and beyond.

Number cards in a 'light bar' format.

Language

Number names, higher, lower, order, lowest, highest, between, more than, fewer than.

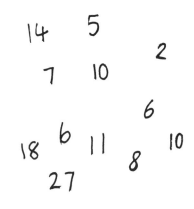

How it fits

With topics

Part of a topic on numbers.
Part of a topic on size.

With National Curriculum

- Making and monitoring decisions.
- Developing mathematical language and communication.
- Developing mathematical reasoning.
- Developing an understanding of place value.

What next?

Larger numbers.

Recording.

Pick a card as a starting number.

Smaller numbers and negative numbers.

Higher and lower

Ask one of the children to enter a number into his or her calculator. The number can be any number from 5 to 30. The child reveals to the rest of the group the number chosen and throws the bean. If the bean lands painted side up, everyone else enters a number which is higher than the starter person's. If the unpainted side lands uppermost then each person must enter a lower number. Each group member then places his or her calculator on the table, saying the number chosen. When all the calculators are on the table they are ordered at one end of the table according to the numbers on the display. Try to ensure that all the children are looking at them from the same orientation and indicate which end will be used for the lowest number. One of the children can be asked to do this, supported by the rest of the group. As the numbers are placed in order, question the children about the decision they make. Discuss with children the range of numbers within which they feel comfortable to work. Then repeat the activity until each of the children has been the starter person.

HIGHER AND LOWER

Setting the scene

The children will need to be familiar with a calculator prior to this activity. Nevertheless, they will probably want to play with the calculators and will need some time to do so, before you start the activity. It is helpful to have a number line nearby, to help children with the ordering task. You may also find it helpful to make a set of cards with the numbers in calculator style and place them in order on the table for reference. You may wish to limit the range of numbers which the children can choose, e.g. not higher than 50 or 100. If you want to provoke some interesting discussion, allow any starting number. The possibility then arises of a child choosing the number one and the bean landing on 'lower'. This activity is suitable for a small group, working initially with you, but later on their own.

Making and monitoring decisions

As they arrange the calculators in order the children will be making and monitoring decisions. If one child does the organising, the others can observe and comment on the process. Alternatively each child can decide where to place his or her calculator and all of the children can be involved in checking that this is done correctly.

Developing mathematical language and communication

The calculator offers the chance for you to observe children's understanding of the size and order of numbers and of the terms 'higher' and 'lower'. The children also have the opportunity to use these terms in combination, e.g. 'This number is higher than two, and lower than six.' Their discussion when they try to place the calculators in order and the way that they respond to your questions will allow you to note their use of appropriate vocabulary and their reasoning.

Developing mathematical reasoning

The activity provides children with the opportunity to recognise simple numerical relationships. Verbalising their reasoning is very difficult for young children. Your careful questioning and prompting can enable them to express their ideas more clearly, e.g. 'What made you decide to move this calculator to that end?' 'How did you know that?' You may wish to extend the children's reasoning by asking questions such as 'What would happen if we put in a very large number?' 'Will we always be able to put in a number that is larger/smaller than . . .?' 'How can you be sure?'

Developing an understanding of place value

Children may count, to verify the ordering. They will be using the number names. They may have the opportunity to recognise sequences. They will be reading and ordering numbers and developing an understanding that the position of a digit signifies its value. The children's responses to some of the questions identified in the section above will enable you to ascertain their understanding of this essential concept. You can also ask, 'Have we got a number that is higher than 37 and lower than 52? How would you know by looking at the digits?' The activity gives you a chance to find out if any of the children know about negative numbers.

HIGHER AND LOWER

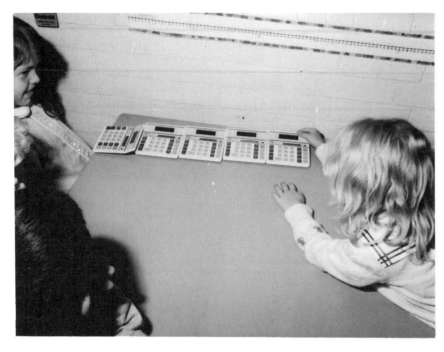

What might happen

This activity allows children to select numbers with which they feel confident. Observe whether the children are more able to work with small numbers than large ones.

Some children may not be able to choose an appropriate number to put into the calculator to make it higher or lower as required. This may be because they have difficulty with ordering the numbers. Alternatively, they may not be able to input the number they want. For both of these difficulties it is helpful to direct the children's attention to the number line and discuss which numbers come before and which after. Emphasise the words higher and lower in relation to the number line. If the children are not managing the task with large numbers, you may, in discussion with the children, want to reduce the range of numbers under consideration.

Some children may find it difficult to recognise the number symbols in the calculator 'light bar' format. Draw their attention to the set of number cards on the table and support them through the activity. Make a mental note that these children will need additional experience to familiarise themselves with these symbols. (See Calculator numbers.)

Some children may show that they are able to order the numbers, but not be able to explain their reasoning. Hearing other children's explanations will help them to develop the appropriate language skills. You might ask them, 'Will using the number line help you to explain?'

Children who are confident with this activity will enjoy their knowledge and skill and may enjoy including numbers higher than the range, and even negative numbers. Ask them more demanding questions requiring them to verbalise their reasoning.

Links with other activities in this book:

Calculator numbers (page 26)   Handfuls (page 6)
Number ladder (page 22)

Supporting children's learning

Children who have difficulty with ordering numbers

You will need to offer activities that will help these children to develop a mental image of the counting numbers in sequence, so that they can deal with ordering numbers that are not consecutive. These children will be supported by always having available number lines and number grids for their individual work. It is also important that number lines and number grids are displayed in the classroom for both children and teachers to use, e.g. when discussing the attendance in class each morning.

HIGHER AND LOWER

More specific tasks with the number line and grids will help them focus on numbers in sequence, e.g. they can make their own, fill in the missing numbers, find the number before and after (higher and lower than) a given number, arrange a shuffled pack of number cards (8–13, 0–10 etc.) in sequence. More demanding tasks should be given where the numbers to be put in order are not consecutive, e.g. 7, 1, 3, 11, 19. There are a number of games using packs of numbered cards to support this aspect of ordering, e.g. Tricksy (Count Me In pack: ILEA 1985). This uses a pack of cards numbered 0–100 which are dealt to the children so that they have six each. In turn, each child selects a card from her or his hand to place on the table. The aim of the game is to win the trick by putting down the card with the highest number.

Audio tapes provide excellent opportunities for children to use and extend their mental image of numbers in sequence. You can make your own tape; for example, reciting the numbers 0–100. You can then ask the children to use this to locate a number picked from a 0–100 pack of cards. The children will need to decide whether to wind the tape forwards or backwards and by how much. Another tape could set children mental challenges such as, 'Imagine a number line in your head. Find the number six. What does it look like? What number comes before/after? Find a number which is higher. What is it? Describe to your friend and/or record what you have seen.'

Children who have difficulty with recognising and writing numbers

The activities listed above will support these children. However, they also need to focus on reading and writing numbers and understanding place value. Set up a display where children can see numbers written in different formats and scripts. The children can contribute to this display by making numbers using a variety of materials, such as matchsticks or Plasticine.

Children who cannot explain their reasoning

Encourage children to explain to each other what they have done in as many mathematical situations as you can. Activities such as 'I'm thinking of a number' require the children to reason. In 'I'm thinking of a number' the children offer suggestions to which you might reply 'too big' or 'too small'. It is helpful to have a number grid to hand so that the children can work out which numbers can be eliminated. You can ask them to explain their reasoning: 'How did you know that?'.

Extensions

The range of numbers can be extended into three digits. The starting number can be provided by turning over a card from a pack containing three digit numbers. If a die is provided it can lead the children to investigate the concept of negative numbers or fractions. Questions such as 'Is there a number smaller than one?' may prompt children into this investigation. In all of these activities children can be asked to record their findings.

Play 'Box It', a strategy game where children have to decide how to place numbers in sequence. You need a track containing ten spaces and a set of number cards (e.g. 1–50). Shuffle the cards and deal ten of them, face down. The child turns over one card at a time and decides where to place it on the track. Once a card has been placed it cannot be moved. The aim is to place all the cards in the correct numerical sequence.

SECRET NUMBER

What before?

Early level: experience of counting, simple operations with objects, writing numerals.

Later level: experience of some or all written number operations.

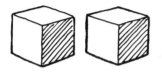

Resources

Sticky notes.

Paper.

Coloured pencils.

Counting aids: cubes, calculators, number lines.

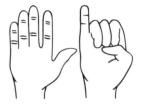

Secret number

Give each child and yourself a sheet of paper with a sticky yellow note in the middle. Colour your own note as a house. Write your secret number underneath. Draw or write appropriate clues to the secret number around the house (sss and sss, 3+2+1, 8 take away 2, 20–14). Can the children suggest more clues for your number without revealing what the number is?

The children each make a house, write a 'secret number' (from five to ten) underneath and put down as many clues as possible around the house. Discuss with the group and then challenge the whole class by displaying the children's work.

Note: This activity can be done with the whole class with you using a note on a flip chart to model the problem.

Language

Number names.

Add, subtract, multiply, divide.

How it fits

With topics

Part of a topic on homes.
Part of a topic on numbers.

With National Curriculum

- Making and monitoring decisions to solve problems.
- Developing mathematical language and communication.
- Developing mathematical reasoning.
- Understanding relationships between numbers and developing methods of computation.

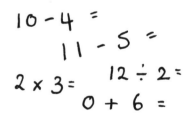

What next?

Different number.

Larger number (door number?).

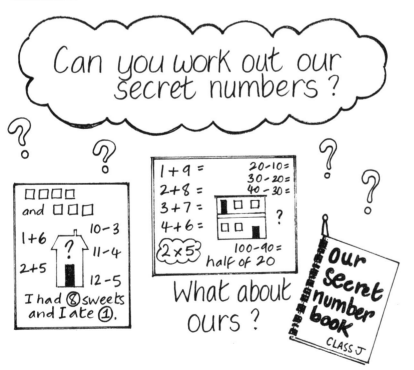

SECRET NUMBER

Setting the scene

When you model the activity with the group or class make sure the children know that they are not to reveal the secret number until they have been asked. Put down no more than two clues initially. Then invite the children to offer some of their own. Encourage them to check that each clue has the secret number as its answer. The clues that you offer can be used to extend the children's mathematical approaches and representations. The children can be left to work on their own secret numbers, with occasional encouragement, support and challenge from you. They can then challenge a partner to work out their secret number.

Making and monitoring decisions to solve problems

The openness of this activity allows the children many opportunities to make decisions.

- the children will be selecting the mathematics they wish to use and are able to use;
- they can decide what materials and equipment will best help them;
- they can be challenged to develop a different approach to the problem by observing your original examples and those of other children.

Looking at the children's clues to their secret number will help you to make an assessment of their problem solving and numerical ability.

Developing mathematical language and communication

This activity offers the children a purpose for recording mathematics. They also need to interpret other children's recordings. From both of these you will be able to assess the extent to which the children can read and understand the meaning of mathematical symbols.

The children will use a variety of forms of presentation: drawings, number and word sentences; showing the number itself; or any of the four number operations according to their understanding of these.

Developing mathematical reasoning

This activity could encourage children to begin to use simple patterns and to make predictions as to how the pattern might continue.

Understanding relationships between numbers and developing methods of computation

The main focus of this activity is for the children to explore how numbers can be juggled around. What relationships do they have to each other? Can you add or take away different numbers and still get the same secret number? Playing with numbers in this way can lead to understanding inverse operations, e.g. that subtraction is the inverse of addition, and also to deepening children's understanding of relating patterns in our number system.

SECRET NUMBER

What might happen

As this is an open-ended activity there will be many different responses depending on children's range of ability, experience and level of confidence.

During the whole group session, some children may be reluctant to offer suggestions. This could be because they are naturally quiet or are unable to think of a suitable clue. You may decide to encourage the quiet ones by direct questioning or to just allow the children to observe and listen to other children's clues.

Some children may offer incorrect clues to your secret number. Try to be sensitive in your response to these children and check the clues with them in a quiet way rather than just rejecting them. It is important that each child feels that his or her contribution is valued. If you are not sensitive the child may withdraw from offering suggestions in the future.

During independent work, initially the children need to make their note into a house, which means that *all* the children can begin the task. This will give you the opportunity either to home in on those you feel will need support or to work with other groups of children.

A few children may be reluctant to put down any clues to their secret number. You could suggest that they look at the clues you wrote together for some starting ideas. You could point out the counting aids available to them in the classroom and ask if they want to select one of these to help them. If they are still reluctant help them to get started by devising a clue together.

If the openness of the task is threatening to some children, try to present them with a challenge that is appropriate to their ability. For example, with a less able child you might say, 'I want you to make up *three* clues for your secret number.' For a more able child you might set a higher limit.

Some children may not realise that the secret number is the 'answer' to the clues, e.g. if the secret number is five they may put put '5 and 1 = '. These children are not really ready for doing this activity independently. Make a note of this to be followed up later.

Some children may produce clues which are all of the same type, e.g. addition. Draw their attention to the variety of clues you devised together, perhaps focusing them on extending their choice of operation, for example, subtraction.

Finally, children who are confident with this activity may begin to use simple patterns, e.g. 13 – 4 =, 14 – 5 =, 15 – 6 =, and with careful questioning could

SECRET NUMBER

make further predictions, e.g. 'What would you write next?' and eventually 'Could this go on forever?' or 'What would happen if your clue started with 100 – ?'

Links with other activities in this book:

Ladybirds (page 10)   Rosie the hen (page 14)
Number ladder (page 22)   Higher and lower (page 30)
Calculator numbers (page 26)   Handfuls (page 6)

Supporting children's learning

Children who do not realise that the secret number is the answer

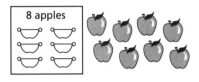

8 apples

These children need lots of experience of making number bonds with a variety of concrete materials to begin with, e.g. 'In how many different ways can you put eight apples into two baskets? In how many different ways can you arrange nine playpeople in three train carriages?' You need to encourage the children to record, either in their own way or by providing a format for recording.

This could involve number sentences if the child is ready for it, but drawing would also be appropriate. There are many similar ideas in Workjobs 2 by Baratta Lorton (1979) but it is easy to make up ideas yourself based on your current topic.

These children would also benefit from working on similar activities on the number line, e.g. 'How many ways can the frog do two hops to ten?'

Frog drawing

Children who produce clues of the same type

These clues are usually additions and children need the chance to explore the other operations with concrete apparatus, number lines and calculators, e.g. 'Pick a card from a pack numbered 10 to 20. How might you get to number 7?' After the children have used concrete materials, encourage them to do a similar task using the number line and the calculator.

Extensions

Children who begin to use simple patterns (usually subtraction patterns) could be encouraged to choose a different number as their secret number. Later they can choose a two-digit number as their secret number.

Other 'equivalence' activities can be given to challenge the children. 'What other additions will give you the same answer as 19 + 5? Are there different subtractions which will give you the same answer as 21 – 4?' These can be mental tasks for the children to work on.

Children can explore the multiplication facts of a number. 'How many different rectangles can be made with 12 cubes? Is there a pattern in the multiplication facts? What other multiplications will give the same answer as 6 × 4?'

The children can use the calculator to extend their patterns into large numbers.

FEELY BAG PAIRS

What before?

Experience of sorting and matching.

Feely bag pairs

Ask each child in the group to find a pair of identical objects, each pair being different from the others. Each child puts one of the pair into a 'feely bag' and leaves the other item on the carpet.

Can each child find his or her own object by feeling inside the bag?

If you describe what you are feeling in the bag, can the children identify the 'partner'? Ask each child in turn to identify the partner of an object you describe. The feely bag and objects can then be made available for the children to continue matching the pairs. New pairs of objects can be introduced and the 'expert group' can introduce new children to the task.

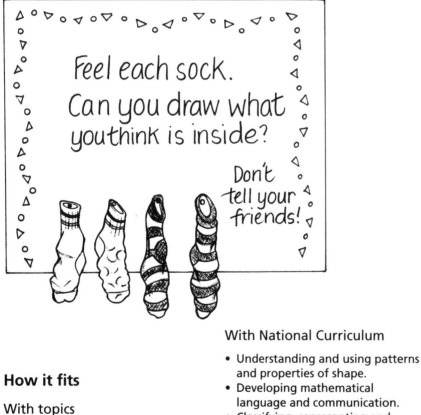

Feel each sock.
Can you draw what you think is inside?

Don't tell your friends!

How it fits

With topics

Topic on senses.

With National Curriculum

- Understanding and using patterns and properties of shape.
- Developing mathematical language and communication.
- Classifying, representing and interpreting data.

Resources

A large drawstring bag.

Everyday objects, e.g. balls, dolls' shoes, plastic cups, wooden bricks, pencils, duplo, shells.

Language

Identical.

The same/different.

Curved, straight, rough, smooth, large, small etc.

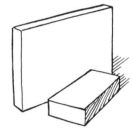

What next?

Ask the children to describe the objects.

Draw a plan of each of the objects. Can the children match their objects to the plan? Can they look at the plan of an object and find it by feel?

Use different sets of objects that you have chosen, e.g. some that are the same shape but different sizes, a set of balls that are of different sizes or textures.

Put individual objects into individual socks (old but not holey!). Can the children draw what they think the object might be?

Use shapes that will focus on more specific mathematical properties, such as faces and edges.

FEELY BAG PAIRS

Setting the scene

Initially you will need to work either with a small group or with the whole class to introduce them to this activity.

You will need to discuss what you mean by the word identical. For some children the colour of the objects will need to be the same, as well as the size and shape, although others may appreciate that colour does not really matter in this case. You may want to describe each of the objects before it is placed into the bag or ask the children to describe them in order to begin to develop a shared descriptive language.

Understanding and using patterns and properties of shape

The specific focus of this task is to help children to visualise and describe 3D objects. Because the children are using everyday objects, with which they will be familiar, they should develop the skill of picturing them relatively easily. As you are initially doing the describing, this will help the children to develop their range of language. Their skills can then be developed and refined with less familiar, more mathematical objects at a later stage.

Developing mathematical language and communication

During the initial stages of this activity you can begin to assess the children's understanding of descriptive language. Your intervention will help to develop this understanding and eventually refine it so that it becomes more focused on key mathematical properties such as curved, straight, long, short. Your modelling will help the children to gain confidence in their own powers of description, which you can encourage at a later stage.

Classifying, representing and interpreting data

By identifying identical objects the children are using skills of sorting and classifying with a particular focus on shape and space. In trying to identify an object from your description they are interpreting data.

FEELY BAG PAIRS

What might happen

Children may not be able to find an identical pair of objects even after you have discussed the meaning of the word. If they bring objects which are exactly the same apart from the colour, you may decide to pick this up at a later stage? However, if they bring two objects which *only* have colour as the common property they are not really ready for this activity but may benefit from looking at the identical pairs that the other children bring to the activity. In this situation you may decide to accept the child's choice so that he or she does not feel left out; you will need to be prepared to discuss the difficulty of identifying the object by feel. If this is not appropriate you may give that child a pair that you have already sorted out, so that they can actually take part in the activity at this time.

Because the children have chosen the objects, it is unlikely that they will be unable to find their partner by feeling in the bag. However, if this should occur it may be that the children did not understand that they had to find their *own* object and they can be given another try. If they continue to choose any object, put all the objects back in the bag and let the child have another turn when there are only two objects left in the bag.

If you talked about the objects before they went into the bag the children should not find it too difficult to identify the objects from your description. It is difficult, however, as the describer, not to talk about colour, as you can see the partner that is on the carpet. If some of the children do have difficulty with your description it may be that your language is too far removed from the children's and you may have to modify it initially, making it more precise as the children become used to the activity.

Some children will have no difficulty with any aspect of this activity but will enjoy their success and will benefit from the refinement of language that you can introduce when describing the objects. They can also be extended by being encouraged to be the describer if you feel it is appropriate.

Links with other activities in this book:

Dolly mixtures (page 66)   Towers (page 50)
Boxes (page 42)   What's missing? (page 74)

Supporting children's learning

Children who need more help with matching identical objects

Where children cannot find pairs of identical objects they need to be given the opportunity to focus on activities which require them to match pairs of objects. Initially there should be obvious differences between the pairs of objects and those which are not to be paired. The differences between each pair should then become more subtle. Use 3D objects, 2D objects and pictures to support this.

Children who have difficulty with identifying an object by feel

It may be helpful to set up situations where there is only one hidden object that they have to feel. If, as above, the object to be identified is initially very different in shape or size from the rest of the set which *is* in sight, this will

FEELY BAG PAIRS

help. The child will gain confidence and should be able to distinguish more subtle differences at a later stage.

For example, initially put a table tennis ball in the bottom of a family size yogurt pot and place them inside a sock. Have another table tennis ball outside, together with a pencil, a piece of Lego, a book etc. Later you might have the same ball inside but outside have a tennis ball, a marble, an apple, a plastic cup etc.

Children who cannot identify an object from your description

It may be, as suggested in 'What might happen', that you need to be more specific in your language. It can be difficult to describe an object that you know well in language that is clear and unambiguous, e.g. 'How might you describe a cup?' More structured shapes, e.g. Logic Blocks, can be useful here, but only if you have had a lot of discussion about the objects before they are hidden. It may be that some children just find it hard to listen to a list of things. Focusing on developing their listening skills in everyday classroom activities will be helpful here, e.g. story time, music time, following instructions in PE.

Developing the children's skills at describing objects should be an ongoing classroom activity. Encourage them to play carpet-time games such as 'I'm thinking of something', describing it to the class so that they can identify it. It does not have to be something that is in the classroom. It may be something to do with the topic you are doing at the time, e.g. a spider, or a ladybird.

Extensions

In some ways it is harder to get the children to describe an object when they are doing this activity than it is when they are imagining something, like a spider. They need to concentrate closely on the specific attributes of shape, texture and size but not to reveal the name of the object. However, some children will delight in the challenge and most will improve if the activity is made available for them to do whenever they want.

Instead of having pairs of objects you could make little cards with the outline or plan of each of the objects that is in the bag and do the activity trying to match object to plan. This can be as challenging as you want, depending on the objects and their similarity.

BOXES

What before?

Some experience of 3D shape.

Some experience of the language associated with 2D and 3D shape.

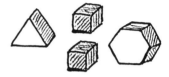

Sorting recyclable materials, constructing boxes from clixi, geostrips, straws.

Boxes

You will need a collection of interestingly shaped boxes.

Ask each child to choose one box and say one thing about it.

Ask questions about the shapes of faces. Note the children's use of appropriate vocabulary and their understanding of words such as cube, cuboid, faces, edges and vertices.

Play Kim's game. Hide the boxes under a cloth and ask one child to remove a box. When the remaining boxes are revealed, the other children describe the missing box.

Allow each child to choose a box from a 'consumable' collection. Ask them to talk about the reasons for their choice and to compare their choice with other people's. Ask them to count the faces and to describe the shape of each face (using 2D terminology).

For the next part of this activity ask the children to paint the faces of their box. (If you can bear the mess, a different colour for each face.) Make an instant and interactive display by mounting the printed papers with the boxes on a shelf below. Discuss the display with the group, then invite the rest of the class to work with the display from time to time.

Resources

Collection of boxes.

Consumable boxes for printing: cube or cuboid.

Paint: thickly mixed.

Large sheets of paper.

Language

Shape names and properties, e.g. edges, vertices, faces, square, rectangle, triangle, circle, cube, cuboid, prism, pyramid.

How it fits

With topics

Part of a topic on shopping.
Part of a topic on packaging.
Part of a topic on shape and space.
Part of a topic on boxes.

With National Curriculum

- Making and monitoring decisions to solve problems.
- Developing mathematical language and communication.
- Developing mathematical reasoning.
- Understanding and using patterns and properties of shape.
- Understanding and using measures.

What next?

Different shaped boxes.

Working with nets of boxes.

Match the net to the box.

Making boxes.

Play 'I'm thinking of . . .'

BOXES

Setting the scene

This is a teacher-intensive activity, at least until the children are familiar with Kim's game. You will need to work with a small group. By choosing a box yourself you can introduce the children to the language of face, vertex, vertices, edge and the names of 2D and 3D shapes. As each child makes a statement about his or her shape you can make an initial assessment of the use of mathematical language. You can then progress to asking specific questions like 'How many faces/edges/vertices has your shape got?' or 'What shape are the faces?'

The display of children's printing from the second part of this activity should be interactive. Place the boxes on a table top and arrange the printed papers, each with a lace attached, behind the display. Ask questions such as 'Which printing matches which box?' and encourage any child in the class to use the laces to make the match.

Making and monitoring decisions to solve problems

In the printing activity the boxes represent mathematical equipment and provide the children with the opportunity to use them to explore the properties of 2D shape (the faces). The printing task also requires them to organise their work. You should ask them to check that they have printed using every face and have not duplicated. The idea of using a different colour for each face helps the children (and you) to check.

Developing mathematical language and communication

Each stage of this activity requires the children to understand and use the language and properties of shape. As the children describe the missing shape, encourage them to use mathematical language, rather than brand names and colours. It is important that children start using the correct terms to distinguish between 2D and 3D shapes. Throughout this activity children will be responding to mathematical questions which you have posed. They have the opportunity to ask mathematical questions and discuss their work.

Developing mathematical reasoning

By careful questioning you can emphasise the relationships between boxes which are different examples of the same 3D shape, e.g. a matchbox and a toothpaste carton. You might ask, 'Are any of these boxes the same in any way? What is the same about them? What is different?' In discussing relationships between the printed patterns and the boxes in the display the children can begin to understand general statements such as 'All the faces on a cube are squares', 'All cuboids have six faces.'

Understanding and using patterns and properties of shape

The specific focus of this task is to provide opportunities to describe and discuss shapes. Kim's game requires them to visualise the shape and then describe the image. Predicting the shape which will be printed by a face also demands visualising, which is an important part of all geometric activity. Requiring the children to focus on similarities and differences supports them

BOXES

in classifying shapes according to mathematical criteria. As the children describe and discuss the shapes they will need to recognise and use geometrical features.

Understanding and using measures

As children focus on the differences they notice they are likely to comment on comparisons of length and perhaps volume.

What might happen

Children may talk about the boxes without using any specific mathematical language. This may be because they are not familiar with the terms, or it may be that they know the language, but have not yet incorporated it into their own repertoire. They will be supported by hearing you and other children using mathematical language, and by responding to questions such as 'How many faces has your box got?' or 'Which shapes are on your box?'

Children may answer incorrectly the questions about the properties of shapes. One reason for this may be that they find it difficult to count the number of faces, vertices or edges. To do this successfully children need to do a careful one-to-one count, remembering where they started and what faces they have already touched. You can help them by touching each face or edge as they count aloud and checking, 'Is there a face we haven't counted yet?' You will need to decide how much emphasis you want to put on to this aspect of the task. It may be appropriate simply to count together and then move on to the next section of the task.

Some children find it difficult to visualise. Kim's game involves the use of visual memory, and some children may not be able to identify which box is missing. You may give a prompt like 'I can see *one* box with triangular faces . . .'

Children may make all kinds of error in the printing activity for a variety of non-mathematical reasons. They may have difficulties with their motor control or retaining the purpose of the activity as they get involved in the sensual pleasure of working with paint. You will need to keep reminding the children that they should print once with each face, particularly if you are intending to use the finished works of art for display purposes. Ask questions such as 'Which face are you going to paint next?' 'What colour will you use?' 'How many faces have you still got to paint?'

Some children will be able to use appropriate language, count the faces, ascertain missing boxes and print successfully. They can be extended within

BOXES

the task by contributing ideas for the display of their work and communicating their findings to the rest of the class.

Links with other activities in this book:

Towers (page 50)   Handfuls (page 6)
Feely bag pairs (page 38)   Dolly mixtures (page 66)

Supporting children's learning

Children who are unable to use the specific mathematical language

Here they need a variety of experiences which will require them to use mathematical terms. Ask the children to make models with construction materials like Polydron and straws and to talk about their constructions, preferably to an adult. Children may also be asked to contribute to a display or to create pictures based on a particular shape. Again make sure that they have an opportunity to describe what they have done to you or to the rest of the class.

Children who find it difficult to visualise

Many aspects of this activity require the children to be able to visualise the shape of the box. This is a specific skill which can be developed. As a first step to helping children to abstract the properties of shape, set out a variety of shapes on a table (these could be a set of 2D or 3D shapes, but not a mixture) and ask the children to picture one shape in their mind, then question them about the properties of the shape. An example is:

How many edges has your shape?
Are they all the same length?
How many faces has your shape?
What shape are the faces?
What is the name of your shape?

The next step would be to ask similar questions about a shape that you have instructed the children to visualise, without the support of the objects in their sight, e.g. 'Imagine a triangle . . .' The children can be asked to manipulate the image of the shape, e.g. 'Make it bigger/smaller', 'Turn it upside down,' 'Turn it back again.'

They can even be asked to cut bits off the shape. 'What are the properties of your new shape?'

Extensions

Play 'I'm thinking of a box', where the children have to ask questions which will help them to identify the box you have in mind. This game can be adapted to 'I'm thinking of a shape', where the shape may be 2D or 3D. Children could write their description of a box for other children to guess.

Ask the children to design their own nets and make them into boxes. They could use polydron or card shapes to help them to plan and visualise the finished shape. Provide the children with a collection of different 'nets' so that they can predict and then find out which can be made into boxes.

Children can be asked to design a box to a set of specifications, e.g. 'Make a box just large enough to contain six sweets.' Use Unifix or Multilink cubes to represent the sweets.

COMPARING CONTAINERS

What before?

Some experiences of pouring and filling containers with sand.

Some experience of playing games.

Resources

A small tray (tidy tray) of dry sand to be shared between two children.

About ten small containers (egg cups, large lids etc.), each identified by a different letter or other symbol.

Ten small cards marked to match the containers.

A die with three faces displaying the words 'holds more' and three faces displaying 'holds less'.

Language

Holds more/holds less/holds the same.

Full/empty.

How it fits

With topics

Topic on packaging, shopping, containers.

With National Curriculum

* Developing mathematical language and communication.
* Developing mathematical reasoning.
* Understanding and using measures.

Comparing containers

This is an activity for two children.

Each child picks up a card from the pack, then finds the container which matches the card. They compare the containers to find out which holds more by filling one with sand and pouring it into the other.

The die is then thrown. If less is indicated the child whose container held less sand wins a counter; if more is indicated the child whose container held more wins the counter. The cards are put back in the pack, this is shuffled and the containers are returned to the pile. The activity is repeated until one child has five counters.

What next?

Use containers which look very similar.

Use a specific unit to compare the containers, e.g. teaspoons.

COMPARING CONTAINERS

Setting the scene

Even though you may have sand and water freely available for the children to use, most children will use these in a creative or dramatic way rather than in a mathematical way. Before you start this activity it is useful to have a discussion with the whole class, introducing specific vocabulary related to capacity (full, empty, holds more than, holds less than). Use a tray of sand and a variety of containers and ask questions as you fill and empty the containers, e.g. 'What will happen if I pour the sand from this container into that one? Will it overflow? Will the sand from this container fill the other one? Will there be any space left? Which holds more?' You can then introduce the game to the whole class, demonstrating the way it is played with a child as your partner. By using a small tray of sand and not setting up the activity in the normal sand-tray you can help the children to focus on the task at hand rather than associating it with creative play. The game can then form one of a set of activities which children take turns to play at a table. Alternatively, if you have enough resources, you could set up the game for a number of children to play in pairs. After your initial introduction it is possible for the children to work on this activity without continual intervention.

Developing mathematical language and communication

This activity encourages the children to develop and understand the vocabulary of capacity. By listening to the children's responses during the discussion you will be able to determine their familiarity with and use of this specific mathematical terminology. While playing the game the children will need to recognise the words 'holds more' and 'holds less' and be able to match the symbols on the containers and cards. They will also be continuing to use the comparative language to which they have been introduced.

Developing mathematical reasoning

During the discussion the children are asked to predict what will happen when one container of sand is poured into another. The need to predict continues throughout the game. Although the children can work on their own you may wish to intervene at intervals to determine if their predictions are becoming more accurate.

Understanding and using measures

This activity is focused on the very early stages of measuring capacity, requiring the children to compare two objects directly. In measurement of length it is possible to make direct visual comparisons, but with capacity this is not possible. It is necessary to use something like sand as an 'intermediary'. This means that the child needs some understanding of 'transitivity': understanding that the quantity of sand gives you a way of comparing the capacity of the two containers.

COMPARING CONTAINERS

What might happen

If you have sand and water freely available in the classroom the children will be very familiar with the materials you are discussing. However, some children will not be able to participate in the initial discussion. They may not have enough experience with the materials to know what will happen, or they may be unable to verbalise their ideas. Make a mental note of those children who appear to be unable to contribute. They will benefit from listening to other children's responses and to your explanation.

During the initial discussion some children may be able to respond using language such as 'full' and 'empty' when comparing the containers, but may not be able to understand the terms 'holds more than' and 'holds less than'. It seems obvious to us that if you have poured a container full of sand into another container and there is still space in that second container then the first must 'hold less sand'. However, many children find this concept difficult. Try asking, 'If both containers are full of sand which one holds more?' or 'If each was full of sweets which one would you rather have? Why would you choose that one?'

Some children may have difficulty matching the symbols on the cards and containers. As this is an integral part of the game you may decide not to choose these children to play the game until they have had more experience of matching drawn symbols.

Some children may have difficulty reading the words on the die. Pairing a 'reader' with a 'non-reader' can help here.

Some children may have difficulty playing the game sensibly. Having only a pair of children playing removes the confusion and frustration of taking turns which may arise with playing games. Allowing friends to play together can also help, as they will often support each other.

When playing the game some children may still have difficulty with comparing the containers to find out which holds more or less sand. You may decide to let the misconception go if neither child realises the mistake, and you can address it at another time. You may decide to intervene and support the children if you wish them to complete the game and develop their concept of comparison.

Some children may find the game easy. They will still enjoy the challenge of using their knowledge and skill in a game format and can be encouraged to play some of the extensions when they have succeeded with the first game.

COMPARING CONTAINERS

Links with other activities in this book:

Handfuls (page 6)   Boxes (page 42)

Supporting children's learning

Children who take no part in the introductory discussion

These children should be encouraged to explore filling containers in their structured play with either sand or water. The structure may be provided by restricting the items in the sand or water to containers which encourage pouring and filling, e.g. teapots, cups, plastic bottles and beakers, or by setting a specific task, e.g. 'I want you to find out which cup would be best for Baby bear, Mother bear and Father bear and come back and tell me how you decided.' When talking to the children about what they have done it is important to use the specific language: 'holds more than/less than/the same/full/empty'. You could also encourage the children to report to the whole class and note if they use any of the appropriate language.

Children who cannot say which containers hold more or less

These children may have been helped by the questioning suggested in the 'What might happen' or may have begun to develop the concept while playing the game. If they need further support this might take the form of filling and comparing containers in a variety of contexts, e.g. treasure boxes or pouring out drinks at a party. Games or activities can be used which require children to select the larger container, e.g. the target of the game could be to collect the most gold (sprayed beans or rice). A selection of small containers is offered. The two children race around the treasure island on the board and when they pass the treasure chest they can choose one of the containers, fill it with gold and keep it. The game is over when all the containers have been filled. The child with more 'gold' at the end is the winner. You could ask the children to decide how to find out who has more (they will probably suggest weighing) or you could suggest they compare by tipping all of their 'gold' into a large container one at a time and then look at the different levels reached.

Extensions

The game can be extended by providing a range of containers which look as if they hold about the same, so that the children will need to be more careful with their pouring and filling when making the comparisons.

The cards can be used to select a container and the children can estimate how many teaspoons or scoops they think will fill that container. This might be an activity for an individual or a pair of children. Each child can take it in turns to find out how many spoons the container holds and the child whose estimate is closer keeps that container.

TOWERS

What before?

Some experience of working collaboratively with a partner.

Some experience of 2D and 3D shape.

Some experience of solving practical problems.

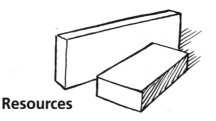

Resources

A selection of small cuboid boxes or bricks, e.g. toothpaste boxes, variety-pack cereal boxes, poleidoblocs.

A3 or A2 sheets of paper, pencils.

Multilink cubes or other 'non-standard units' for measuring.

Language

Names of shapes and their properties, e.g. cuboid, cube, face, square, rectangle.

Height, higher, lower, taller, tallest, shorter, shortest.

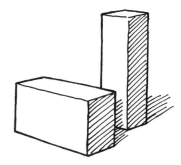

Towers

Give a group of children a selection of small boxes to build with, on the carpet.

Then focus the activity by allocating each pair of children a set of three small cuboid boxes.

Ask them to use all three boxes to make a number of towers, each with a different height. How many different towers can they make? After letting them investigate for a while ask the children how they know the towers they are making are of different heights. Encourage them to think of ways of remembering all the different towers they have made.

Use Yasmin's boxes.
Can you make a tower taller than Yasmin's?

this tall

How can you be sure?

How it fits

With topics

Part of a topic on buildings.
Part of a topic on packaging.

With National Curriculum

- Making and monitoring decisions to solve problems.
- Developing mathematical language and communication.
- Developing mathematical reasoning.
- Understanding and using patterns and properties of shape.
- Understanding and using measures.

What next?

Start with one box: how many towers? Two boxes: how many towers?

Different shaped boxes, e.g. all cubes, a mixture of shapes.

Different numbers of boxes.

Use the boxes to make a building that covers the greatest/least area of table.

TOWERS

Setting the scene

For the initial part of this activity you could let the children explore the boxes while you concentrate on another group. It is likely in this case that they will try to build the tallest tower they can, either on their own or with a partner. Ask them how they decided to build in the way they did before you begin the more focused activity of building with a limited number of boxes. Note the language the children use to describe both the individual boxes and the towers they build. Once the children have been given the more specific task you can stay with them to question them closely about what they are doing, or you can leave them to try to solve the problem for themselves, returning later for them to feed back their ideas to you.

Making and monitoring decisions to solve problems

The children are faced with the problem of ascertaining the height of the towers they create and ensuring that the different combinations give towers of different heights. They will need to organise and check their work and may find the need to record their work. Asking 'Do you think that you have found all the different height towers you can?' will challenge them to try to be systematic.

Developing mathematical language and communication

In discussing and describing the towers the children will need to use the specific language associated with properties of shapes. They will be involved in responding to and asking questions, and they will need to find some form of recording and presenting their work.

Developing mathematical reasoning

The children will need to recognise the relationships between the different dimensions of the boxes and can be encouraged to ask questions and predict what will happen as they are combined in different ways. Careful questioning can be used to help the children to make general statements. For example, 'How do we each make the tallest possible tower?' should prompt children to think about using the longest side of each box.

Understanding and using patterns and properties of shape

The children will need to describe and discuss aspects of their boxes and they should be encouraged to use the appropriate terminology: faces, vertices, rectangles, squares, cubes and cuboids. (Remember that cubes are 'special' cuboids, just as squares are 'special' rectangles.)

Understanding and using measures

The children may compare objects by direct comparison, drawing each tower 'to scale', or they may use non-standard or standard units. They may, for instance, choose to use their smallest box as a unit of measure. 'This box is three matchboxes long and two and a bit matchboxes wide.'

TOWERS

What might happen

While the children are exploring the boxes on the carpet they will already be thinking about the properties and names of the shapes they are working with. By questioning them and asking them to talk about what they have built and how they decided to do it, you will be helping them to make this thinking more explicit. If they do not use the appropriate mathematical terminology, now is the time for you to build on what they do know and extend their knowledge and vocabulary.

When you focus the activity on building with only three boxes, the children may think that there is only one tower that can be made with their boxes, and feel they have completed the set task very quickly. You may decide to illustrate some of the different ways of making the tower, using your own set of boxes if you feel the children need that support.

Some of the children will only find one or two towers even after you have supported them. You may decide that for these children this is enough, and you could then encourage them to find a way of recording the two different towers they have made.

Some children will be able to build lots of different towers, some of which may be of different heights, but some may just be different arrangements that are the same height. Again you need to ask the children to find a way of remembering which towers they have made and how they are different.

The children may have difficulty with deciding how they will remember the towers they have made. The activity requires the children to find a method for tackling this but some may not be able to do this at all. There are several things you might do: provide them with some extra identical sets of boxes so that they can make their different towers and partially complete the task; show them how they could lie their tower down on a piece of paper and draw around it; or let them observe the other children's ideas and decide which they will choose.

Some may decide to do drawings. This will not, of course, show that the towers are different heights, but you may decide that you will accept what the children have done and address the height issue later.

Others may use Multilink cubes or other 'non-standard units' to measure each tower and write down a set of numbers. This will show that different height towers have been made, but will make it very difficult to remake the towers and to know that you have found them all. Again, you may decide to intervene and discuss this with the children or you may leave it until later.

A number of the children will realise that either they have to draw each tower

TOWERS

to scale so that they have a record of how each tower is made *and* how tall it is, or they need to draw each tower (not to scale) in addition to measuring it using a non-standard or standard unit.

It is unlikely that any of the children will be able to find all the different height towers, as there are 27 (3 × 3 × 3) if the three dimensions of the boxes are clearly different. But they may begin to be systematic and you can build on this at a later date (see extensions).

Links to other activities in this book:

Boxes (page 42)   Egg boxes (page 78)
Unifix towers (page 82)

Supporting children's learning

Children who find it difficult to tackle problems which require them to make a number of decisions for themselves could be supported by setting problems with more clearly defined targets.

Children who cannot find more than two solutions

If you have large wooden blocks available, give the children three sets of identical blocks and ask them to build towers of different heights, using one block from each set for each tower. If possible use blocks where the dimensions are very different, so that the height differences are emphasised. When a number of towers have been built, ask the children to talk about their work.

Children who find difficulty with recording their findings

It is helpful to find a reason for recording the children's findings. You might contrive this by asking the children to record their work today, so that they can talk to the class the following day. Covering the faces of the boxes with coloured paper or marking them with symbols will help the children to identify the faces they have used. Use the same colour to identify identical faces.

Extensions

Children who devise their own ways of measuring with standard or non-standard units can be encouraged to refine their methods. Further experience with a variety of measurement tasks should be provided.

Where childen are beginning to be systematic in their approach to such problems, ask them to explore the problem with just one box, then two boxes. This will help them to establish a clear idea about the way in which the problem develops and the most able children will see a way to find the solution by reasoning it out.

Introduce a cube as one of the boxes. How does this change the outcome? What if there were two cubes? Three cubes?

What happens if we increase the number of boxes. How many different towers will be possible?

After exploring linear measure (height) with the boxes, the children can also consider making buildings that cover the greatest or least area of the table. Children can be very creative with this task.

ROBOTS

What before?

Counting.

Experience of left and right.

Resources

Left and right stickers for hands and/or shoes.

Language

Forward, backward, right, left, turn, numbers including quarter, half, quarter turn, half turn, right angle, rotate.

Robots

Sit the children around in a circle in the hall or the carpet area.

Tell them that you are a robot and that you can only move if given very specific instructions. You only understand forward, backward, right, left and numbers. Ask the children to give you instructions to get from the chair to a target which will require several different movements, including at least one change of direction.

Encourage them to be precise in their instructions by 'misunderstanding' them if they are not sufficiently detailed, e.g. if the children say 'Go forward' keep walking forward further than they expect.

The children will need to give you further instructions which are more precise, e.g. 'Go backwards four steps.' Similarly, if the children say turn, you could turn a quarter turn in the wrong direction and they will have to decide how to correct your position.

Continue until you reach your target.

Discuss with the children the decisions they had to make.

Repeat the activity, with one of the children being the robot, and selecting a different target.

Can they successfully instruct the new robot?

How it fits

With topics

Topic on machines.
Topic on journeys.
Topic on toys.
Topic on *The Iron Man* (by Ted Hughes).
Topic on local environment.

With National Curriculum

- Making and monitoring decisions to solve problems.
- Developing mathematical language and communication.
- Developing mathematical reasoning.
- Developing an understanding of place value.
- Understanding and using properties of position and movement.
- Understanding and using measures.

What next?

Recording instructions for the robot.

Setting more difficult targets for movement.

Using Roamer, Pip or other programmable toys.

Giving instructions for everyday activities, such as putting on shoes and socks.

Logo.

Tell the **robot** how to get to the head teacher's office.

Start
door
- turn right
- forward 6 steps
- turn right
- forward 2 steps

START POINTS

Where are you?

Make Roamer go around the carpet.

ROBOTS

Setting the scene

Be prepared for the children to get very excited about this activity!

This could be the children's first experience of work on programming. It offers them an opportunity to give and follow instructions. When it is the children's turn to be the robot you will have the opportunity to observe their abilities in giving and following instructions.

Making and monitoring decisions to solve problems

The children have to solve the problem of how to get you to the target and so may have to overcome difficulties concerned with visualisation and giving clear instructions using restricted language. They will also have to decide which of two or more suggested movements is the best option to take and why.

Developing mathematical language and communication

The children will be required to use and understand specific language related to position and movement in space. They will also be discussing their decisions and refining their language.

Developing mathematical reasoning

In order to instruct the robot to get from one place to another the children may be making a mental hypothesis, e.g. 'I think that if the robot moves forward five steps and turns right it will get to the window.' The child may be engaged in this mathematical reasoning but you will only know if this is the case if her or his instructions lead to the target. There will probably be more than one way to reach the target. Where the children are clearly making a choice between two options, ask them to give the reasons for their decision.

Developing and understanding place value

Children will be given the opportunity to count orally. The work might be related to a number line on the floor or wall of the classroom.

Understanding and using properties of position and movement

This activity requires children to recognise movement in a straight line and rotations, and to describe these movements. It is an ideal opportunity to introduce the idea of angle as a measure of turn. As the children rotate in role as the robot, they experience turning through the required angle. If the pathway is marked on the floor in chalk, you can discuss the size of the angle through which they have turned, e.g. quarter turn, half turn, right angle. You can invite the children to combine movements by asking them to give the full set of instructions to reach a carefully chosen target. This is the equivalent of writing a *procedure* in LOGO or for a programmable toy, rather than using individual instructions.

Understanding and using measures

The children will be visualising, estimating a distance and then predicting how many steps will be needed. The steps are being used as a non-standard unit of length. Similarly, they will be visualising the amount of turn needed and finding a way to express this.

ROBOTS

What might happen

Some of the children may have experienced working with a programmable toy such as Pip or Roamer in an informal setting. In this more structured activity it may be the experienced and confident children who will make the initial contributions. Make a mental note of those who contribute and the extent of their understanding. It would be appropriate to choose one of the more confident children to be the next 'robot'. During the part of the activity when a child is the 'robot' you may find that more children will be willing to give instructions, as they become familiar with what is required of them.

Some children may not contribute at all. This may be because they do not understand the concepts involved in the activity or because they are reticent. If you know that the children are normally reluctant to participate you may wish to encourage them to offer an instruction. Alternatively, you could ask them 'What do you think?' following another child's instruction. Whether the children contribute or not, they will gain from hearing the other children's suggestions.

Some of the children may make inappropriate contributions. This may be because they have difficulty with estimating how far a certain number of steps will take the robot. Alternatively, they may have problems with left and right turns.

Some children will not see the need to refine the instructions, finding it difficult to recognise that what is in their head is not what you hear. You may need to emphasise the way in which machines can only follow orders, not make their own decisions. When the children are playing the role of the robot, make sure that they follow the instructions completely, continuing until they are told to stop.

There may be children who give clear precise instructions. They will still benefit from the opportunity to verbalise their mental image and help others to clarify their ideas.

Links with other activities in this book:

Number ladder (page 22)

Supporting children's learning

The children who do not contribute or who do so inappropriately need experiences of structured play to support:

- skills in estimating length;

ROBOTS

- understanding of turning and applying the appropriate language of right and left;
- ability and confidence to give verbal instructions.

The experiences suggested below will provide the opportunity to develop these, but the children need to verbalise what they have done in order to maximise the learning that has taken place. This could take place at carpet-time with the whole class, or the children could explain the task for others to follow their instructions. Alternatively, you could participate in the 'play', challenging the children with specific questions.

Set up a child-size maze if space allows. This could be in the corridor, hall or playground for individuals or pairs of children to explore. You could use a set of large wooden blocks. The children can then explain how they navigated the maze or give each other instructions for getting through it. If little space is available, a smaller maze can be set up to be used with cars or other toys in a similar way. This could be in the sand-tray, with Plasticine or Lego on a table or with large bricks on the carpet.

If you have access to a programmable toy such as Pip or Roamer the children can be free to explore what it can be made to do.

Ask the children to instruct a visitor to reach the secretary's office. Record the instructions and make a drama activity of the scene.

A play mat marked with roads and other features can prove a useful resource. The children can play freely with the mat, using cars to explore routes. To provide a more focused activity ask the children questions such as 'How can you reach the Post Office from the school?' Children can be asked to work together on a challenge, then report their findings to the class.

PE activities can be linked with this work. Games and activities where children have to follow clear instructions, turning and moving in a straight line, will help them to develop the skills identified above.

Extensions

Children who are confident with giving and following instructions can be encouraged to find a way to record a set of instructions for a partner to try out.

Targets can be made more difficult by choosing one which is not immediately visible (e.g. beyond a doorway). Alternatively, you could choose a target which can be reached by more than one route. Is there a shortest route? Is it possible to return by a different route?

Once children have experimented with Roamer, Pip and other programmable toys, challenges can be set. Simple tracks or mazes can be constructed which require the children to refine their programme through trial and error. Ask the children to explain how they tackled the challenge and overcame any difficulties. Ask the children to explain how they would use what they have learnt to help them solve a different maze.

Ask the children to give a list of instructions for everyday activities such as opening a carton of fruit juice, putting on a hat and coat or getting up in the morning.

The robot activity is one which forms an ideal preliminary for beginning work on Logo. Children who are able to work confidently with the activities suggested above can be introduced to Logo activities, using a floor or screen turtle.

WRAPPING PAPER

Before

Copying and continuing patterns.

Physically creating patterns from assorted materials, turning and sliding.

Associated PE activities.

Talking about patterns.

Wrapping paper

Make a collection of wrapping papers and display them in the classroom. Choose one piece and describe it to the children, using positional words and identifying significant aspects of the pattern. Ask questions like 'Where can you see the next shape like this? Where does the pattern start all over again?'

Ask the children to choose their favourite piece and describe the pattern on it. Pointing to the pattern, ask them questions like 'Are these the same or different? How are they different? What is the same?' (You might want to record the words they use.)

Using the materials you have selected, design a very simple motif (preferably asymmetrical), of which 12 copies will be made. Use these 12 units to create the block for a wrapping paper design. Ask the children to describe the pattern you have made. Could they suggest other arrangements? What if . . .? The children then design their own motifs and with their 12 copies create their own block designs.

Afterwards they can describe their own designs and devise questions for their friends to answer.

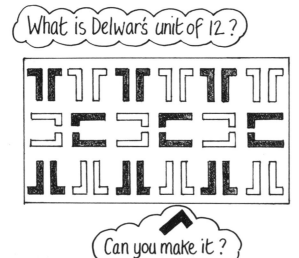

Resources

A collection of wrapping papers showing different ways of repeating patterns.

Potatoes, polystyrene tiles or card and string for printing.

Paper and pencils.

Templates to aid drawing.

Photocopier.

Language

Use of appropriate language to describe pattern.

Position language: up, down, turn, round, across, below, above, slide, drop, under.

Same, different.

How it fits

With topics

Part of a topic on pattern.
Part of a topic on design and fabric printing.
Part of a topic on packaging.
Part of a topic on shape and space.

With National Curriculum

- Making and monitoring decisions to solve problems.
- Developing mathematical language and communication.
- Developing mathematical reasoning.
- Understanding and using patterns and properties of shape.
- Understanding and using properties of position and movement.

What next?

Further work on translation, rotation and symmetry.

WRAPPING PAPER

Setting the scene

You will need to have given the children considerable experience of working with pattern in advance of this activity. Examining patterns in a variety of media, describing the patterns, noting similarities and differences will all help to clarify for the children the idea of a repeating pattern. This is a sustained task and at various stages you will need to work with the group, as it is important to observe them carrying out the activity. By modelling the activity yourself you can feed in the idea of keeping the design very simple. It also gives you a chance to make an initial assessment of the children's use of language, fine motor skills and understanding of the relevant spatial concepts.

Making and monitoring decisions to solve problems

The activity is open-ended, providing the opportunity for children to:

- select the mathematics they wish to use (they might, for instance, decide to rotate the motif, or to slide it up the page);
- organise their work and check how the pattern repeats.

By observing the children and discussing their work with them you can assess their ability to organise their work. Some children may form a plan (orally), others may verbalise the pattern as they progress. Not all children will see a need to check their work. By asking them to describe the pattern to you, you may prompt them into developing a checking procedure.

Developing mathematical language and communication

Children gradually progress from using everyday language to acquiring the language which is specific to mathematics. They also develop more precision in their use of terminology. They should be encouraged to be clear in their description of the pattern.

Developing mathematical reasoning

During the activity children will have the opportunity to recognise simple patterns in their own and other children's work. While you are modelling the activity you can ask the children questions which will require them to predict what will come next, what will happen if . . .?

Children might be encouraged to make general statements, such as 'The star will always be next to the moon shape.' 'The sideways shape is always below the upside down one.'

Understanding and using patterns and properties of shape

The children will find their own ways to discuss the patterns and shapes, but can be encouraged to use specific mathematical language, following your example.

Understanding and using properties of position and movement

Children will be using translations, rotations and (possibly) reflections as they proceed. They may also use diagonal, horizontal and vertical movements, quarter turns or half turns. You can introduce this formal language, but might also want to use slide, turn, flip, slope, across, above, below, clockwise etc.

WRAPPING PAPER

What might happen

Through the discussions that have taken place in setting the scene for this activity it will become evident which children can continue a pattern in a line and which children are also able to see that patterns can be set out in a block and then repeated.

A child will make decisions about the shape of his or her motif and its use in the design on artistic grounds, rather than mathematical considerations. It is very natural in activities of this kind for artistic considerations to take precedence over mathematical ones. However, the mathematical thinking can be extracted by careful questioning at the end of the activity.

Children may find it difficult to design an asymmetrical motif. Ask the children to observe what happens to the shape when it is rotated through 90 or 180 degrees or reflected. Does it look different? If not, can they change the shape so that you can tell it has been rotated or reflected.

Children may compose a block which has no obvious system within it. Where children have no obvious system encourage them to talk about their work, describing how they moved their motif. It would be helpful to them to listen to other children describing their patterns.

As children describe what they have done, you may become aware of a system which is not recognisable from the visual image, e.g. the child may describe the pattern below as 'Up, down, up, down, up.'

While praising the correct pattern established by the child, you can point out the lack of system in the 'ups' and the 'downs', asking her or him if there are any aspects she or he would like to change. These children will also benefit from listening to other children's descriptions.

Some children may be able to create a systematic pattern, but not be able to articulate their system. These children will benefit from hearing you describing their pattern. You might start the description, then ask them to continue. Ask other children in the group to spot the pattern and describe it, to re-emphasise the language.

Some children may be able to work systematically and describe their pattern.

Links with other activities in this book:

Jumps and hops (page 18)

WRAPPING PAPER

Supporting children's learning

Children who are not yet able to recognise patterns in a block formation

These children can be given a variety of media to work with, e.g. pegboards, Unifix pattern boards, tiling generators, ATM mats, tessellating tiles or pattern blocks. Their own linear paper patterns could be cut up and rearranged into a matrix formation. The number of columns chosen will affect the final pattern.

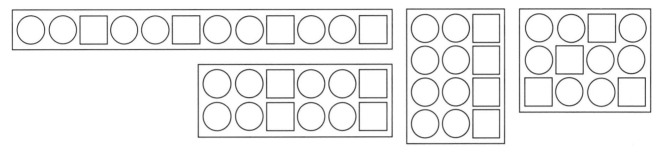

Chanting patterns, clapping patterns and moving their bodies in time with the chant can all help children to establish a firmer idea of continuity and repetition. The use of a range of sensory approaches will ensure that all children have access to these ideas (see Baratta Lorton 1976).

Children who find it difficult to design an asymmetrical motif

Activities which focus on the symmetry of shapes will help them to establish the concept of asymmetry. Children can be asked to complete the other half of pictures and shapes, either by drawing or by using a mirror. Can they draw or create a picture which does not have symmetry?

Children who do not appear to have used a system in their block

Children who are not working systematically will benefit from further work on repeating patterns using a variety of media. They may find it difficult to use the idea of rotations to create a system. It is helpful to provide further experience of rotating shapes, using potato prints, some letters of the alphabet or animal shapes (asymmetrical shapes).

Extensions

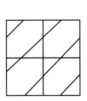

Children can be asked to find a way to record their pattern, or to 'tell someone else how to make your pattern.' They could use their block in different ways to make wrapping paper (e.g. the block could be rotated or translated to continue the pattern). They could create other blocks by using their friends' motifs, or designing new ones of their own.

Further work on rotation, translation and reflective symmetry will build on the experiences in this activity. Children can be given ATM tiling generators, or asked to design a square tile with which they can explore how many different patterns they can make. Restricting the pattern to a block of four tiles will make this more manageable. The number of patterns will depend on the symmetry of the tile. Ask the children to work with tiles that have four lines of symmetry. How many different patterns can they make? (There is only one!) What about a square tile with two lines of symmetry?

HERE COMES THE DUSTCART

What before?

Some experience of free sorting and explaining.

Resources

Collection of interesting clean rubbish (about 40 items).

A dustcart (a toy or box).

Cards for labels.

Language

Same, different, difference, set, sort, belong, not . . . language of justification: all, sure.

How it fits

With topics

Part of a topic on toys.
Part of a topic on journeys.
Part of a topic on transport.
Part of an environmental topic.

With National Curriculum

- Developing mathematical language and communication.
- Developing mathematical reasoning.
- Classifying, representing and interpreting data.

Here comes the dustcart

Tip out the rubbish on to the carpet.

Let the children ask questions and talk about the items.

Ask how the rubbish might be sorted.

Collect a set yourself.

Can the children discover your criterion for sorting?

Make a label to identify the set.

The children all have a turn making a set for the others to guess. A label is made each time. Play 'Here comes the dustcart'. Each child except the driver has a share of the rubbish. The driver selects a label and drives around to collect all the rubbish satisfying that criterion. When the collection is finished, the other children are asked to justify the inclusion or exclusion of some of the items. The other children take turns at being the driver and making the selection, which can then be discussed as before.

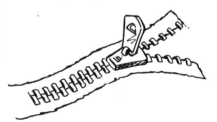

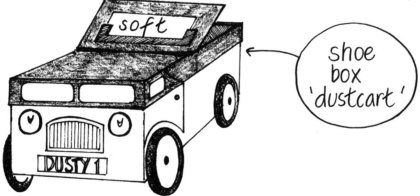

shoe box 'dustcart'

What next?

Play the game with the label concealed, so that the other children have to discover the criterion being used.

Use the same collection to sort in different ways, e.g. boxes to represent bottle banks. Introduce different ways to represent the data: Venn diagrams, Carroll diagrams or tree diagrams (see Appendix).

Is there any item that could go in more than one set?

HERE COMES THE DUSTCART

Setting the scene

You will need to work with the children to introduce the activity, but once they are familiar with the activity they can be left to continue and to show others how to play. As the children discuss their ideas you will be able to focus on the language they use, assessing both their language competence and their understanding of sameness and difference (i.e. early logic).

When making the labels you need to be very specific, e.g. if the children say that their set is the red set they usually mean 'has red on it'. This needs to be clarified with the child and the label must be made appropriately.

Developing mathematical language and communication and developing mathematical reasoning

The activity will generate its own discussion, some aspects of which are directly mathematical, but some which are more general. You will need to focus discussion quite strongly on the reasons for selection of the set. Your own choice will model the type of set which might be chosen.

Children often focus first on colour, so you might choose one type of material, e.g. plastic or wood. The labelling activity serves the purpose of directing the children's attention towards the criterion chosen. This can be emphasised by the following type of questions: 'What is the same about all of these objects?' 'Why did I put this in my set?' 'Could I have included this?' 'Why is that?'

It is important to generate the opportunity for children to use negative criteria as well as positive. 'Why doesn't this one belong in the set?' 'Because it's *not* plastic.'

All of these questions will help children to understand and make general statements, e.g. '*All* of these items are magnetic.' However, you can further emphasise this by asking questions such as 'Why can't *any* of these go into the set?'

You may need to be persistent in your questioning, to encourage the children to justify their ideas in a logical way. For example, where the set selected contains items which all have some red on them, children can be asked why an item does not belong. The answer 'Because it's plastic' is clearly not logical, but 'There's some blue on it' is not a sufficient reason either. Eventually the child needs to establish that the reason the item doesn't belong in the set is that it does not have any red on it.

Classifying representing and interpreting data

The main focus for each child is on sorting, re-sorting and classifying everyday objects. When guessing which set has been made by the teacher or by their friends, they have the opportunity to interpret data.

HERE COMES THE DUSTCART

What might happen

Initially the children will enjoy playing with the objects and talking about them. This is an essential part of the activity, as they are exploring the properties of the objects in their own way. You can listen to their descriptions and this will offer you clues for how you might classify the objects in your own modelling.

Some children will have difficulty identifying your set and making a set for themselves. You may decide to continue to include them, as the dustcart game should support them in developing their understanding in a non-threatening way. It is, however, important that you still involve them in the questioning, both directly and indirectly, encouraging them to listen to other children's responses.

Some children may have difficulty with suggesting another way of sorting, especially if the more obvious categories have already been chosen. You might acknowledge the difficulty and ask if they would like some help from you, and then whisper an idea to them. Alternatively, you could show them the labels that have been made already and ask them if that helps them to think of another idea.

Some children will be able to classify with ease. This activity gives them the opportunity to be inventive and to extend the range of criteria and accompanying language. This can be supported by your offering an unusual classification, e.g. transparent, or a combination of two criteria, e.g. green and plastic.

Links with other activities in this book:

Dolly mixtures (page 66)   Fabric beanies (page 70)

Supporting children's learning

Children have difficulty in describing your set

This might be because they do not understand that they are looking for a similarity in each of the items or because they do not have the language to describe it. It may not be possible to identify which of these problems is the case. Further experience of playing or watching the game will support their development. You can provide a more directed activity by preparing a pack of

HERE COMES THE DUSTCART

cards with different properties. Give the children cards and ask them to collect a number of items for the property on each card. The children describe their items and say what is the same about them all. They should also watch other children's selections and try to decide which card they chose.

Children who have difficulty suggesting other ways of sorting

Play Dolly mixtures. Use the children themselves as items to sort, making sets based on different criteria. Play 'gatekeeper' games, where the gatekeeper holds a question card, e.g. 'Are you wearing red?' Children are only allowed through the gate if the answer is 'Yes'.

Play 'Can I cross your golden river?' Mark a line on the floor. One child is the river child. The other children ask, 'Can I cross your golden river?' The river child answers, 'Yes, if you're wearing lace-ups' (etc.). Continue like this, thinking of new criteria, until all the children are over the river. You can use the same technique to dismiss the children at the end of a session.

Carefully planned and structured simple surveys (e.g. 'Do you like lightning?' as part of a weather topic) can support children in their understanding of classification.

Prepare a clear collection chart (a Venn diagram, a tree diagram or a Carroll diagram) and a blank label for each child's name. The information gatherers can stick the label on to the appropriate part of the collection chart according to the responses to the question. You can follow this up by devising a question for your chart, e.g. 'Which children like lightning?' In this way all the children can become involved in interpreting the data gathered.

Extensions

Sorting activities have been criticised in recent years. There may have been an overemphasis on simple sorting activities, so that children have been expected to continue with activities which were not challenging for them. Our view is that sorting is a basic skill, essential to data handling activities and providing the opportunity for reasoning and the development of logical operations. Once children have shown an ability to identify a common property they can be offered a range of activities to challenge their reasoning. The introduction of sorting diagrams will help them to bridge the gap between concrete and abstract representation. These can take the form of games, such as those suggested above, where the children can walk along a tree diagram or sort themselves into a Carroll diagram or Venn diagram.

A further extension can be to consider data which require more complex forms of classification. The dustcart activity may lead to questions about the intersection of two (or more) sets. Such data can be represented in the diagrammatic form and questions based on 'both . . . and' can be asked, e.g. 'I am thinking of someone who is wearing *both* a watch *and* a belt.'

Games such as 'What's in the square?', using a matrix formation, can be very useful for extending the ideas above. These activities can be very complex and demand a high level of reasoning skills. You will need to develop children's skills gradually. You will need a set of attribute cards logically arranged in the matrix. Secretly remove one card, then ask children to identify what is missing from the matrix. Alternatively, children can play 'I am thinking . . .' where they think of a card and the other children try to find out which card they have in mind.

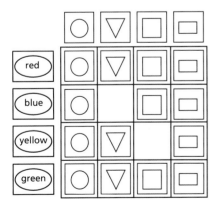

DOLLY MIXTURES

What before?

Some experience of free sorting and describing sets.

Resources

Dolly mixtures.

One large paper plate.

A small paper plate for each member of the group.

Language

Shape names and properties.

Colour names.

Same, different, difference, set, sort, belong, both . . . and, all not.

Dolly mixtures

Put the dolly mixtures on a large plate in the middle of the table.

Collect a set of sweets for yourself and put it on a small plate in front of you. Ask the children if they can describe your set. *Do not* put your set back.

Give each child a small plate. Ask each child, in turn, to take a set of sweets from those remaining on the big plate, explaining why they have chosen those particular sweets.

Can each child in the group make a different set if each time a set is chosen it is *not* returned to the big plate?

Can you go round the group, with each child collecting a second different set from those remaining on the big plate?

How it fits

With topics

Topic on food.
Topic on shopping.

With National Curriculum

- Developing mathematical language and communication.
- Developing mathematical reasoning.
- Understanding and using patterns and properties of shapes.
- Classifying representing and interpreting data.

What next?

Sort the dolly mixtures in a different way.

How many sweets in each set?

Compare numbers, weight.

Are there any sweets that could go in more than one set? More than two sets? Record the sets made.

DOLLY MIXTURES

Setting the scene

You will need to work with the group and listen carefully while they do this activity, as the emphasis is specifically on discussion, and if you are not there the children will eat the data! The children will need time to talk about the sweets. Allow them plenty of time for this, so that you can assess the language they are using. As they talk, you can listen and note the language they use and the properties they notice. It might be useful to have a notebook with you to jot down key words and phrases. These brief notes will help you with assessment and allow you to develop the children's language using their own starting points. It will also enable you to retain ideas and issues which you may wish to raise later in the discussion.

Developing mathematical language and communication

From the children's talk you will be able to identify the mathematical vocabulary that the children seem to understand and are confident to use. There may be vocabulary you wish to refine. For example, a child might say, 'I'm collecting the rounds', which would be the opportunity for you to feed in the mathematical terms cylinder and/or sphere. You might also draw the children's attention to the properties of those shapes by asking questions such as 'What is the same and what is different about your choice of sweets?' It is important that the children have the opportunity to use mathematical language when talking to you and each other.

Developing mathematical reasoning

Sorting and classification tasks are specifically about recognising mathematical relationships. As children identify similarities between the sweets they choose, they are showing their awareness of these relationships. The activity also requires them to respond to and ask mathematical questions about the criteria for their classification. In the Introduction we discussed how children can develop mathematical reasoning when they need and want to work things out for themselves. Dolly mixtures is an example of an activity which generated this need. For example, if you ask, 'Can you find me all the sweets which are both pink and made of jelly?' you are introducing the logical connectives of 'both' and 'and'. In order to answer the question, the child has to identify the set of pink sweets and the set of jellies and decide which sweets belong in both sets (the intersection). It may be difficult to tell whether the children are restricted by their reasoning or by their vocabulary, and you will need to observe the children's actions and listen to what they say to make judgements about this.

Understanding and using patterns and properties of shape

By watching the children sorting the dolly mixtures you will gain insight into their understanding of the similarities and differences of 3D shapes. You will need to watch for children who demonstrate their ability to recognise the properties without being able to verbalise their reasoning, as well as those who may not use shape as a criterion or do not appear to have an understanding of shape. Dolly mixtures are made in shapes which can readily be described in specific mathematical language. This activity gives you the

DOLLY MIXTURES

opportunity to introduce or reinforce the names and other properties of both 2D and 3D shapes in a situation which makes 'human sense' to the children, as well as to determine which properties they are already aware of.

Classifying, representing and interpreting data

In Dolly mixtures the children may *classify* by colour, shape, preference, squashiness etc. They will be *representing* their ideas by physically sorting, but may go on to stick their dolly mixtures on to paper plates or draw their sets. Other children can be asked to say how the sets have been made – *interpreting* the data.

What might happen

After the initial excitement you can prompt the children to think more mathematically by questions such as 'What made you decide to include this one? Could this one go in your set? Why can't this one go in your set?' This discussion may be particularly beneficial for bilingual children and children whose language skills are developing slowly. Some children may have limited experience of sorting, which is why we suggest that the teacher chooses the first set. This also serves to establish the pattern of language to be used. For example, *Child*: 'They're all brown.' *Teacher*: 'That's right, they all have some brown in them.'

Some children may not be able to describe the set you made. It may help to select two sweets and ask the child to identify what is the same about them. Alternatively, you could choose a sweet from outside the set and ask the child why he or she thinks it has not been included.

A child may make a set which does not appear to be clearly defined. Ask the child to explain the reasons for the choice. The explanation may help him or her to reorganise the set.

Children often sort for colour in the first instance and may not notice that some of the sweets have two colours. By keeping each set and sorting only the remaining sweets the children will be challenged to consider other properties.

The children may begin to notice that some of the sweets that belong in their sets have already been selected by someone else. If this happens, a discussion might lead to early ideas about the intersection of sets, where one sweet could belong to more than one set. Let the children discuss these ideas and reach an agreed decision. The idea of intersection can be followed up on another occasion.

DOLLY MIXTURES

Links with other activities in this book:

Fabric beanies (page 70)   What's missing? (page 74)
Here comes the dustcart (page 62)

Supporting children's learning

Children who cannot describe a set or who cannot make a clearly defined set

Give the child specific attributes to look for, using both structured and unstructured materials. For a detailed account of ways in which children can be supported to develop these skills see the corresponding page of Here comes the dustcart. A further idea related to Dolly mixtures would be to use small boxes, labelled appropriately, and ask children to be the machine which sorts all of the jellies (for example) into the box.

Children with limited experience of sorting

It is useful to give children lots of sorting experience with classroom materials. These could be lots of different collections of buttons, shells, junk and other non-structured materials, Logic Blocks and home-made structured sets, e.g. fabric beanies (see page 94); and don't forget the children themselves. It is very valuable to do this kind of sorting with the whole class on the carpet, using questions such as those in the 'What might happen' section.

Extensions

If children are already adept at sorting, then they do not need more of the same experience, but should be encouraged:

- to look for more sophisticated attributes (e.g. sweets which are of two colours, sweets which roll, soft/hard sweets, sweets with flat faces);
- to experience more complex sorting;
- to represent their ideas.

You could make labels for the attributes of dolly mixtures which the children have already suggested. Instead of using one attribute the child could use two labels (for example, sugar-coated and will roll) and make that set. This may lead to the empty set if there are no sweets which both roll and are sugar-coated. Alternatively, two children may each take a label and discuss how they deal with the ones which they are both collecting, i.e. the intersection of the two sets (see Appendix).

You will find it interesting to notice how the children record their first experience of intersecting sets. You may find that they initially 'balance' the items on the connecting edge of the two sets or make an attempt to place items straddling the sets. Children at this stage need time to play with the ideas and to develop their own language to express their thoughts. It is not necessary to insist that they use formal mathematical language or standard representation, but *your* use of these will provide models for the children to use as they develop their understanding of this concept.

FABRIC BEANIES

What before?

Developing the language of logic.

Making and describing patterns.

Resources

A logical set of 12 fabric beanies: three different colours, two types of mouth, six light, six heavy (see Appendix).

Language

Light, heavy, position words, e.g. next to, above, below.

Language of justification, e.g. all, sure.

How it fits

With topics

Part of a topic on the senses.

With National Curriculum

- Making and monitoring decisions to solve problems.
- Developing mathematical language and communication.
- Developing mathematical reasoning.
- Classifying, representing and interpreting data.
- Understanding and using measures.

Fabric beanies

Ask children to sort the beanies according to their own criteria. Other children guess the child's criteria. Arrange the beanies logically to form a matrix, but with one missing. Ask children to describe the missing one (e.g. heavy blue beanie with a smiling face.)

Children take turns to hide a beanie and arrange the rest in rows for the others to describe the missing one.

What next?

Domino-type games, where each beanie is different in one way from the next. The child describes each difference as he or she adds a beanie.

Play, 'I'm thinking of . . .'

Use other structured sets.

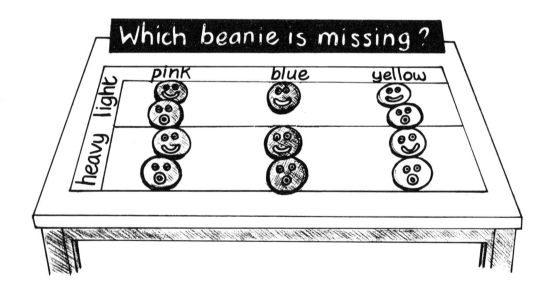

FABRIC BEANIES

Setting the scene

You need one set of fabric beanies for each group (see p. 94). If only one set is available, then groups can work on different tasks and each take a turn with the beanie activity. You will need to work with each group to introduce the activity, but once they are familiar with the activity the children can be left to continue under their own steam. Your assessment of the children through this activity will focus on two main areas: logic and their use of language. An alternative way to introduce this activity initially is to begin with the beanies hidden in a large carrier bag. One beanie is revealed. 'What else do you think is in the bag?' Reveal a second beanie. Ask the children to say what is the same and what is different. Continue in this way, occasionally asking, 'Do you think there are any left in the carrier bag?' Demand precise descriptions of the attributes of the beanie remaining in the bag. If the children think there is a wide mouthed, heavy, yellow beanie in the bag you can then look for and retrieve it. Continue in this way until all the beanies are revealed.

Developing mathematical language and communication

Encourage the children to describe the beanies in words, rather than point to them. The beanies enable the children to sort the materials physically, even if they cannot initially use the appropriate language. The children will demonstrate their understanding by their actions, which will allow you to intervene to develop the appropriate language. An initial discussion of the different qualities of the beanies will introduce the specific language (light, heavy, colour names and description of mouth shapes). You may need to sort the beanies yourself in the first instance, talking through your reasoning as you do so, e.g. 'My set is going to be the wide mouthed beanies. The heavy, blue, wide mouthed beanie can go into the set, but the heavy, pink, round mouthed beanie is not allowed into my set.'

Developing mathematical reasoning

The set of beanies is created as a 'logical set'. There are 12 beanies: three different colours, yellow, blue and pink; two types of mouth, round and wide; and two different weights, heavy and light. Each beanie is different from every other one. The children will need to use these attributes to reason logically when they create their sets and when they 'guess' other children's criteria. Extended experience working with this set of items will enable the children to become familiar with its attributes and to phrase their questions appropriately. At this age there is often a vast range of ability in logical thought between different children.

Classifying, representing and interpreting data

The children will sort and classify using the criteria related to the properties of the beanies, representing their ideas by means of the actual beanies and the sets created. Interpretation will occur when they guess other children's reasons for creating their sets. This part of the programme of study for number is an integral part of using and applying mathematics: developing mathematical reasoning.

FABRIC BEANIES

Understanding and using measures

In sorting the beanies the children will be comparing weights and using the appropriate language.

What might happen

The children will need time to handle and explore the beanies. They may associate bean-filled beanies with bean bags, so you may need to focus their attention on the attributes of weight and texture.

Some children will be able to create a well defined set but not be able to describe it in words. You can introduce appropriate descriptions, but often it is more helpful if other children do the talking. When a suitable description is reached, it may be appropriate to encourage each of the children to repeat it.

Some children will be able to demonstrate that they have understood the construction of the set by adding to it but may not be able to express the criteria in words. Again, discussion is needed to introduce the appropriate language. You may wish to do this or encourage other members of the group to define the set.

Rather than defining a set, some children may 'order' the beanies, listing them 'first favourite, second favourite' etc. You could provide hoops or box lids to contain the sorted beanies, emphasising the need to establish where each beanie belongs. It may be useful to label the sets.

Some children may appear to create a random set, with no apparent rationale. You can remind them of sets which have previously been made by other children and draw their attention to subsequent sorting by other children.

Some children may be able to consider two attributes at a time, e.g. 'All the blue smiley beanies are in my set.' This kind of thinking will help when they progress to working with the beanies arranged in rows. You can introduce the logical connectives to emphasise the fact that two attributes are considered simultaneously, e.g. 'Jasmin's beanies are *both* blue *and* smiley. Can we put this pink smiley beanie in the set? No, we can't, as it is smiley, but it is *not* blue.'

When the beanies are arranged in rows the children have to consider more than one attribute at a time. Some children find this difficult and will concentrate on only one attitude. Encourage the children to look again at the rows and columns to clarify the attribute they have identified and help them to focus on the one they have missed.

Links with other activities in this book:

Here comes the dustcart (page 62)   Feely bag pairs (page 38)
Dolly mixtures (page 66)   What's missing? (page 74)

FABRIC BEANIES

Supporting children's learning

Children who can create their own set but cannot define it, and children who can add items to a set but cannot define the set

Children's language skills develop gradually and their ability to express their ideas through language is acquired through listening to other people. If your assessment of a child leads you to think that it is his or her language ability which is holding him or her back, then carefully grouping the child with others who can express themselves more clearly will lead to gradual improvement.

Children who order the items, but do not put them in a set

You can provide more structure for the activity by giving the children physical barriers to contain the sets. Trays, hoops or box lids will emphasise that a decision has to be made about each item. Labelling the tray or hoop may also help. Concentrate on one attribute at a time and emphasise the '*NOT*' aspect of criterion, e.g. 'All these beanies are blue. All the rest are *not* blue.'

Children who create an apparently random set

It may be helpful to work with unstructured sets. A child who is unable to create a well defined set, and unable to explain his or her reasoning, is likely to need additional support for language and thinking skills. If possible, choose a set of items which has a particular appeal to the child (e.g. animals, cars) and allow plenty of time for discussion before introducing trays, hoops etc.

Children who find the matrix formation difficult

By setting the beanies out in rows you can make the structure of the set more apparent to the children. However, to find the missing beanie they have to consider rows and columns simultaneously. Some children will find this difficult, but it is a good introduction to a method of presentation of data they will encounter later in mathematics. Discuss the content of each row and each column, focusing the children's attention on the similarities and differences within the layout. It is helpful to use a matrix format for other charts and information around the classroom, especially where it involves data about the children themselves, e.g. charts, keeping a record of activities which children have completed, activities which take place on different days of the week, recording sheets for surveys.

Extensions

Children who are able to consider two attributes simultaneously could be encouraged to develop this understanding. Use the beanies to play a domino game, where each player chooses a beanie which is different from the last in the line by just one attribute. A more complicated game can be played where the beanie must be different by two attributes.

Play 'I'm thinking of . . . a beanie which is both yellow and heavy. Can you tell me which beanies it could be?'

The introduction of other structured sets such as Logic Blocks or Compare Bears allows these children to apply their understanding in a different context.

WHAT'S MISSING?

What before?

Experience of playing/working with a variety of classroom resources. Sorting, matching and counting.

Resources

Enough place mats/trays/boxes to separate each of the resources.

Jigsaws.

Packs of cards numbered from zero to nine.

Boxes with lids.

Cups and saucers (from the play area).

Pairs of socks/gloves/shoes.

Subset of Logic Blocks.

Sets of plastic animals, e.g. four each of elephants, horses, cats, ducks.

A set of Cuisenaire rods (one to ten).

Symmetrical pictures (cut in half).

(Any set or collection that has some structure or pattern to it.)

Language

Comparative language, e.g. more, fewer.

Names of objects, numbers etc.

How it fits

With topics

Everyday classroom tidying. The display can be related to any ongoing classroom topic.

With National Curriculum

- Developing mathematical language and communication.
- Making and monitoring decisions to solve problems.
- Developing mathematical reasoning.
- Developing an understanding of place value.
- Understanding relationships between numbers and developing methods of computation.
- Classifying, representing and interpreting data.
- Understanding and using patterns and properties of shape.

What's missing?

Set up a worktable or a display table with a number of resources (see Resources) that have one or two items missing. Put a large label in the middle with the question 'What's missing?' Make notes for yourself of the missing items.

Talk to the whole class about what you have done and say that it will be set up for the whole day (or longer/shorter if you wish) and that the children should take it in turns to try to find out what is missing from each set. Tell them that they should not let other children know what they have found, and you will be asking them how they found out.

At the end of the day discuss what the children have discovered and *how* they found out what was missing.

What next?

Cards numbered 0–20, 0–30 etc.

Dominoes.

Sets with more subtle missing elements.

Number problems, using pictures or symbols.

A display all about '20', for example, but with some sets which have fewer than 20.

WHAT'S MISSING?

Setting the scene

Make sure you know what is missing from each set of resources.

If you are using the starting point for a specific group rather than as an ongoing activity, you will need to make sure that your choice of resources will provide appropriate challenges for the group. You will also need to provide more resources at the worktable than there are children. They will then be able to exchange resources as they complete each 'What's missing?'.

You may wish to remind them occasionally to think about how they ascertained what was missing so that they can report back on their systems. The reporting back will give you an opportunity to assess the children's ability to discover the missing items and describe their methods of discovery. Try to emphasise the notion that there might be more than one way of solving each problem by asking, 'Did anyone work it out in a different way?'

Making and monitoring decisions to solve problems

In trying to work out what is missing the children will be selecting and using the appropriate mathematics, e.g. numerical or spatial skills. They will need to consider different approaches to solve the range of problems and organise themselves accordingly.

Developing mathematical language and communication

Although the tasks themselves are intended to be challenges for individual children, the shared discussion at the end of the allotted time will offer an opportunity for the children to explain what they have done and to listen to other children who may have tackled the same task in a different way. The actual language used will of course depend on the focus of the tasks that you originally set.

Developing mathematical reasoning

All the tasks that are part of 'What's missing?' require the children to recognise patterns and relationships in order to be able to determine what is missing.

Developing an understanding of place value

The tasks that involve working with cards numbered zero to nine, sets of animals, pairs and cups and saucers will involve the children in counting, matching, ordering and checking totals. Working with Cuisenaire or with odd numbers or even numbers that have been selected from a zero to nine pack will focus more on the sequencing aspect of this strand of number.

Classifying, representing and interpreting data

Most of the tasks will require the children to sort and classify the objects involved, and working with Logic Blocks will enable them to focus particularly on the well defined components of a structured set.

WHAT'S MISSING?

Understanding and using patterns and properties of shape

Deciding what is missing from boxes and lids, jigsaws and symmetrical pictures will make the children focus on properties of 2D shapes.

What might happen

Because of the variety of tasks within the activity you can plan it so that every child will have success with some aspects. Children might find it difficult to keep the secret of what is missing once they have discovered it, so you should be prepared to change the missing piece or replace items at an appropriate point. Make a note of what you have changed and record which children have already worked with the task. A list of children's names beside each task may be useful, and the children can tick their names as they complete the task.

For this activity some mathematical learning will take place while the children are doing the tasks at the worktable, but this needs to be consolidated and developed through the quality of the discussion which takes place at the end of the day. When managing this feedback session you will need to consider carefully how you ask the children to contribute. You can target your questions at particular children that you have observed working successfully with the tasks. These may include children who were reluctant to participate, or children who have struggled to complete the tasks, but eventually succeeded.

There will be some children who have been unsuccessful in some of the tasks. Where you have observed that this is the case you can keep a record, noting the mathematical context of the task which each child found difficult. During the discussion these children will benefit from listening to others and they should be encouraged to contribute in areas where they have been successful.

Some children may be able to tackle the tasks, but will find it difficult to explain their reasoning. Some of the relationships may be difficult to verbalise; for instance, finding the missing jigsaw piece is essentially a spatial exercise and the child may respond by saying 'I did the jigsaw and there is one bit missing.' If you have planned carefully which piece is missing you can ask them to describe it, e.g. 'It's the lorry driver's head' or 'It's the corner piece from the top.'

Some children may find a partial solution to 'What's missing?', particularly where the items in the set have more than one attribute. For example, a child might identify that there is a blue Logic Block missing. Asking 'What else can you say about the missing piece?' may encourage him or her to consider size, shape etc.

For some tasks children may have taken differing approaches and have a range of different strategies to offer. You should ask the children, 'Has anyone found a different way to do this?' Be prepared for creative answers! Children who thought there was only one way to approach the task will have their thinking extended by exposure to other methods.

Links with other activities in this book:

Feely bag pairs (page 38)
Boxes (page 42)
Fabric beanies (page 70)

Rosie the hen (page 14)
Ladybirds (page 10)

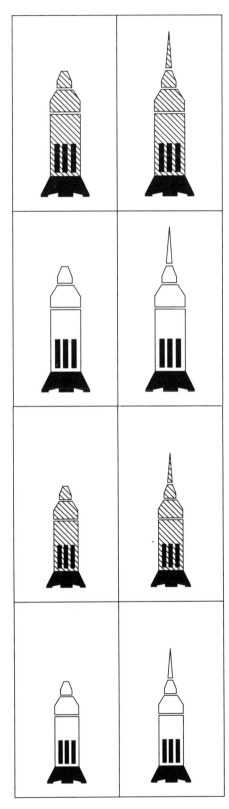

Supporting children's learning

Children who have been unsuccessful in some of the tasks

The tasks suggested for this activity require the children to match, order, sequence, count or classify items or to use their spatial ability. You need to identify the aspect which the child is finding difficult and provide additional experience in this particular area. For example, a child might find it difficult to make pairs from a collection of coloured socks. To help this child to discriminate you may need to provide collections of objects which are more easily distinguished from each other and contain fewer items.

Children who can tackle the tasks, but find it difficult to explain their reasoning

It can be quite difficult for children to explain the reasons for their actions, but learning to justify decisions is an essential part of developing mathematical reasoning. This skill is one which will develop gradually and children will learn from listening to other children's ideas. You can help children to formulate their ideas by specific 'closed' questioning. 'Did you use the picture to help you complete the jigsaw?' 'Did you count the elephants?' 'Were there more elephants than cats?' Questioning children about their reasoning is something which should form an integral part of everyday mathematics.

Children who find a partial solution to 'What's missing?'

This is likely to happen with the activities where the items in the set have more than one attribute. These children will benefit from experience with structured sets. It may be helpful to arrange the items in a matrix formation, which helps to emphasise the logical basis of the set. Some structured sets are available commercially, such as Logic People and teddy bears, but you may wish to make your own sets, related to ongoing work.

Extensions

The nature of this activity is so open-ended that you can increase the level of challenge as you see appropriate. You might decide to make it a permanent feature of the classroom, with the display changing each week.

As the children's familiarity with number symbols increases, you can make the number card activity more challenging by working with larger numbers or creating more complex sequences; for example {3, 6, 9, 12 . . . 18, 21}.

Introduce a number line with one or more numbers missing.

Draw a birthday cake with '6 Today' written on, but with just four candles on top.

When children are familiar with symbolic representation for number operations you can introduce problem cards such as 6 + . . . = 8.

Include a set of dominoes with one piece missing. This can be challenging with a normal 'double six' set. You can reduce the level of challenge by removing all the dominoes with a six or increase it by using a 'double nine' set.

EGG BOXES

What before?

Counting.

Working logically.

Resources

Egg boxes (with six cups).

Plasticine.

Paper and pencils.

Flip chart.

Language

How many?

Different, the same.

More, fewer.

Next to, between.

How it fits

With topics

A topic on food.
Easter.

With National Curriculum

- Making and monitoring decisions to solve problems.
- Developing mathematical language and communication.
- Developing mathematical reasoning.
- Classifying, representing and interpreting data.
- Understanding and using properties of position and movement.

Egg boxes

Give each child an egg box and ask them all to make one egg out of Plasticine to put in the box. Ask the children 'How many ways can you put the egg in the box?'

Discuss what they find and share the different ways, using six-egg egg boxes and/or drawing the different ways on a flip chart.

Then ask each child to make a second egg the same colour as the first. How many different ways can they put the two eggs into the box? Will there be more, fewer or the same number of ways as there was with one egg?

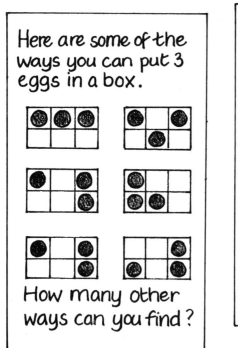

Here are some of the ways you can put 3 eggs in a box.

How many other ways can you find?

Savannah's mum painted 3 eggs for Easter.

How many different ways could she arrange them in the 3 egg cups?

What next?

Three eggs, four eggs etc.

Egg boxes of different sizes.

Two eggs of different colours.

EGG BOXES

Setting the scene

There are two parts to this activity. The first part, using only one egg in the box, should allow any child to participate and it could be initiated with the whole class. For the group work you will need to collect six egg boxes and enough Plasticine for six. Give one egg box to each of six children and use these to model the activity. The activity will be more effective with a small group, as getting the children to make their own eggs and giving each an egg box will help them to focus on the task and make it their own. Sharing what they have discovered about placing the single egg helps to set the scene for the second part of the activity. It also supports those children who found it difficult to find all six different ways, and allowing those children who were successful to explain why there are *only* six ways.

Making and monitoring decisions to solve problems

You may want to model a way of recording the results or you may prefer the children to decide for themselves how they will remember the ways they have found. If you choose the latter you will be able to see if the children can organise and check their work. However, if the children are not used to making such decisions you could use this activity as an example of how they might go about it.

Developing mathematical language and communication

During the activity the children will have the opportunity to discuss and ask questions, using positional language (e.g. next to) and numerical language (e.g. more, fewer). It also allows the children to see and use a variety of forms of mathematical representation, e.g. physical representation of the eggs in the box, written presentations.

Developing mathematical reasoning

By asking children to predict how many ways two eggs can be arranged in the egg box you can encourage them to consider simple relationships and to make predictions about those relationships.

Classifying, representing and interpreting data

This activity provides the children with the opportunity to record their findings in their own way. If you display the recorded findings children then have the chance to interpret other people's diagrams.

Understanding and using properties of position and movement

In order to explain how the eggs can be placed the children need to describe the possible positions. In the course of this they make comments which indicate that they recognise symmetry.

EGG BOXES

What might happen

In the small group the children may want to play with the Plasticine and make lots of eggs (or at least one egg for each hole). This could be something that you allow for some children while you are waiting for all of the group to complete their eggs. They will not be wasting their time as they will be counting and matching and you can use the eggs later to set up an interactive display of the task.

This activity is concerned with arrangements in the box. Comparing relative positions can be particularly difficult as it is to do with visual perception and prior knowledge. Ask the children to explain why they think one arrangement is different from another. You can help by putting the examples the child feels are different beside each other so that they can compare visually.

Some children may not understand what you mean by putting one egg in the box in different ways. They may think that turning the egg over in the same hole is 'different'. Changing your language may help. 'How many different places can you put the egg in the box?' 'How many different holes could you put the egg in?'

In the 'two-egg' investigation some children may think that switching two eggs counts as a different arrangement. You may decide to just note their response and do nothing. It will make no real difference to that particular child's ability to complete the task but may affect the rest of the group. You may decide to open a discussion with the whole group to reach a common 'ruling'.

Some children may find it impossible to remember where they put the egg(s) each time. You could provide them with extra empty egg boxes or pre-prepared record sheets to encourage them to record in their own way.

A child who is confident may not need to use the Plasticine egg(s) or boxes at all but may go straight to pencil and paper to record different positions. These may be correctly represented or there may be repeats. Encourage the children to check each time they draw a new position and not to be afraid to cross out if they have repeated something.

Links with other activities in this book:

Ladybirds (page 10)
Rosie the hen (page 14)

Towers (page 50)
Unifix towers (page 82)

EGG BOXES

Supporting children's learning

Children who find it difficult to organise and check their work

This needs to be developed over a long time, with many different experiences. It is helpful to establish whole school agreement on this approach. Further experience with combinatorial problems will help children develop these skills, e.g.

- How many different numbers can you make using only the digits two and three?
- How many different ice creams can you make if you can have two scoops in each cone and three flavours?
- How many different towers of three Unifix pieces can you make using only red and blue cubes?
- If Shaheen has a yellow shirt, a blue shirt, yellow shorts and blue shorts, how many different outfits can she wear?

For each activity you need to ask, 'How can you be sure you have all the possibilities?'

Focus the children's thinking by sharing the results and emphasising the patterns which they have found.

Extensions

For those children who find the pattern for two eggs and are systematic in their approach, encourage them to think about three, four, five and six eggs. The pattern is in fact symmetrical. There are 6 ways for one egg, 15 for two eggs, 20 for three eggs, 15 for four eggs, 6 for five eggs, 1 for six (1 way for no eggs completes the symmetry).

If you feel this is too difficult you may like to ask them to try a smaller egg box and find all of the options for different numbers of eggs in those, e.g. a four-hole egg box (the boxes can be cut to size).

Note: Braille is based on an array of six dots, each arrangement representing a letter. How many different letters can one dot represent? What about two dots etc.?

UNIFIX TOWERS

What before?

Some experience of sorting.

Some experience of combination problems, e.g. the ice cream problem (see 'Egg boxes').

Resources

Unifix cubes in two different colours.

Sticky paper squares in two colours.

Plain paper.

Squared paper.

Coloured pencils.

Language

The same, different, another, identical, tall, high.

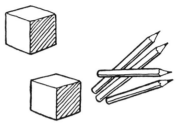

How it fits

With topics

Topic on buildings.
Topic on colour.
Topic on change.

With National Curriculum

- Making and monitoring decisions to solve problems.
- Developing mathematical reasoning.
- Understanding relationships between numbers and developing methods of computation.

Unifix towers

Place a tray containing two different colours of Unifix cubes on the table. Ask one child to make a tower which is three cubes tall. Who thinks she or he could make a different tower three high?

Discuss with the children how the towers are different. Ask them to predict how many different towers of three they could make, explaining their predictions.

Ask them to use the cubes to find out. Can they find a way of checking if they have found them all? Can they find a way of recording what they have done?

At the end of the session ask the children to share their findings.

How many towers 2 cubes high?

with 1 colour   1 tower

with 2 colours   4 towers

with 3 colours   9 towers

What about with 4 colours?

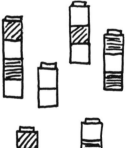

What next?

What if there are four cubes?

What if there are three colours?

Solving other combination problems.

UNIFIX TOWERS

Setting the scene

This activity is most appropriate for work with a group and needs an intensive input at the beginning to focus the children on the limitations you have set. You may decide, however, to let the children explore the cubes in any way they wish, while you initiate work with another group. The children could focus on pattern or they might explore different ways of making a number. Free exploration of the materials is quite valid at this stage. When you do begin to work with the group it is important that you discuss what aspects of the towers are the same ('they are all three cubes tall') and what are different (e.g. the arrangement of the two colours of cubes). You should emphasise that because you are building towers, a red at the top with two blues at the bottom is different from a red at the bottom and two blues at the top.

Making and monitoring decisions to solve problems

The children will be involved in decision making in trying to identify different ways to make the towers. They will need some kind of recording system to monitor the decisions. The record may simply consist of the Unifix towers set out in front of them, or they might use sticky paper squares or squared paper and coloured pencils to record the towers that have been made. If they are used to making their own decisions you can simply tell them which resources are available and leave them to choose how to record. By observing the way in which children record their findings you will be able to assess the extent to which they can work systematically.

Developing mathematical reasoning

The children can be encouraged to explain any patterns they notice and to use them to predict how many towers can be made. They may establish relationships between numbers and justify their ideas, e.g. 'If I can make two reds and a blue, I must be able to make one red and two blues.'

Understanding relationships between numbers and developing methods of computation

Although this is not the main focus, this activity gives the children the opportunity to work with number bonds, finding different combinations to make three.

UNIFIX TOWERS

What might happen

Some children may have difficulty in recognising towers which are the same or which are different. Bringing the two towers together will enable direct comparison to be made. If it is still not apparent to the child, you could ask her or him to 'say' the tower out loud. Point to each cube and ask the child to name the colours in order. Do the same with the second tower. You might repeat this yourself, using your intonation to emphasise the pattern.

In this activity we are using the word 'difference' in a specific way within the context. Essentially, the 'difference' we are asking children to note is the different arrange-ments of the cubes. Some children (particularly those with special needs) may perceive the two towers as different simply because they are made from different cubes.

When asked to predict how many different towers are possible, most of the children will guess. Accurate estimations and predictions are usually based on previous experience. If the children have not experienced this kind of investigation before, they are likely to find it very difficult. If, however, they have worked on 'Egg boxes' or similar problems, they may be able to relate the present problem to their previous knowledge. You should note how realistic the children's guesses are and then ask each of them, 'How did you decide that?' If a child gives the correct answer this may be a guess or a flash of insight, which he or she may or may not be able to explain. It is advisable to leave the question unanswered at this stage, so that the children have a real problem to solve in their investigation.

When the children investigate the problem they may find it difficult to keep track of their solutions. Some children may need help in selecting an appropriate method. Using the cubes themselves is the easiest and most direct way for children.

Some of the children may choose a method of recording which is appropriate, but have difficulty in using it effectively. It may be appropriate to guide them into developing a systematic approach which they can then continue on their own.

A few children will have developed a systematic approach and may therefore be able to establish that they have found all the combinations. Justifying this to you will be extremely difficult for all but the exceptionally able child. The language skills needed for this kind of justification are very sophisticated. You may see evidence that a child is able to reason it through, but is unable to articulate his or her ideas. For example, the child may line up the towers in a way which makes the systematic approach very clear, but be unable to explain what he or she has done.

UNIFIX TOWERS

Links with other activities in this book:

Ladybirds (page 10)   Towers (page 50)
Egg boxes (page 78)

Supporting children's learning

Children who have difficulty in seeing towers which are the same and different

Where children find it difficult to perceive same and different towers, they can be given activities where they are asked to reproduce something exactly. Choose materials like Lego, pegboards, shapes, tiles which the children can manipulate physically. Encourage them to talk about their work and to use the terms 'same' and 'different'.

Children who make wild guesses

Prediction is very difficult for young children, as they do not like to be wrong. Making this part of your everyday classroom practice will help them to develop more confidence. For example, 'How many children do you think will be staying to dinner tomorrow?' 'We've planted 20 seeds. How many do you think will grow into plants?'

Children who find it difficult to keep track of their solutions in a systematic way

These children could be helped to see a purpose for recording if you ask them to 'show and tell' their findings to other children in the class or at assembly. Alternatively, they could be asked to make a book. More experience of problems of this type where the children have to find all possible solutions will help.

Children who find difficulty in justifying their ideas

This is one of the areas where children's mathematical reasoning is ahead of their linguistic skills. Asking children to justify their ideas in a variety of contexts can stimulate the most able children to reason mathematically. The language skills will develop gradually but it might be helpful to verbalise your own reasoning so that the children have a model to work on.

Extensions

If there are children who find the task easy, you could set them the problem of working with towers four cubes high using two colours. The solutions with two colours and an increasing number of cubes are identical to those given in 'Egg boxes'.

An alternative would be to use three colours with towers three high. You need to be aware that in problems of this sort (combinatorics) the numbers increase rather rapidly.

Other combination problems are suggested on page 81 of 'Egg boxes'.

Appendix

Number scripts and symbols from different countries

You may have children who are familiar with counting and recognising symbols from different languages. The following pages may provide a useful reference.

Turkish

1	bir	beer		6	altı	ahl-te
2	iki	eekee		7	yedi	yedy
3	üç	ewch		8	sekiz	sekiz
4	dört	dirt		9	dokuz	doh-cooz
5	beş	besh		10	on	on

Greek

1	ένα	ena		6	έξι	eks
2	δύο	dhio		7	επτά	epta
3	τρία	tria		8	οχτώ	okto
4	τέσσερα	te-se-ra		9	εννέα	ennea
5	πέντε	pende		10	δέκα	dheka

Vietnamese

1	một	mot	6	sáu	sow
2	hai	high	7	bầy	bye-e
3	ba	bah	8	tám	tam
4	bốn	bon	9	chin	djin
5	năm	nam	10	mười	murlh

Mandarin

1	一	yie	6	六	lio
2	二	er	7	七	quie
3	三	sayn	8	八	bay
4	四	see	9	九	jiu
5	五	woo	10	十	she

Gujerati

1	૧	ek	6	૬	chha
2	૨	be	7	૭	saat
3	૩	tran	8	૮	aath
4	૪	chaar	9	૯	nav
5	૫	paanch	10	૧૦	dash

Urdu

1	١	ek	6	۲	chhe
2	٢	do	7	۷	saat
3	٣	leen	8	٨	aath
4	٤	chaar	9	٩	nau
5	۵	paanch	10	١٠	das

Punjabi

1	੧	ik	6	੬	chee
2	੨	doo	7	੭	saat
3	੩	tin	8	੮	arht
4	੪	caar	9	੯	no
5	੫	parj	10	੧੦	das

Bengali

1	১	ek	6	৬	choy
2	২	dui	7	৭	shaat
3	৩	tin	8	৮	aat
4	৪	chaar	9	৯	noy
5	৫	paanch	10	১০	daush

Book to extend Ladybirds activity

Use sticky paper for ladybirds and count out the correct number with the children.

Ask each child to make ten ladybirds out of sticky paper or fewer if it is appropriate. Then either let the child decide how many ladybirds to put on top of and underneath their leaves, or ask each child to put a particular number on top and then put the rest of the ten underneath.

Make all the pages from zero to ten or ten to zero ladybirds sitting on a leaf, and read each page with the whole class. The children will soon join in and begin to predict how many are under each leaf as the pattern emerges.

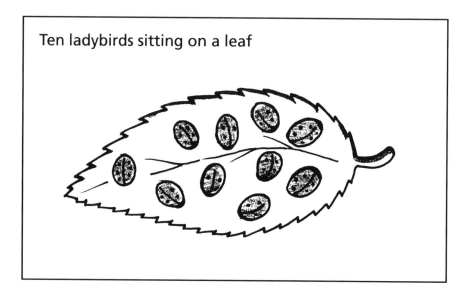

Ten ladybirds sitting on a leaf

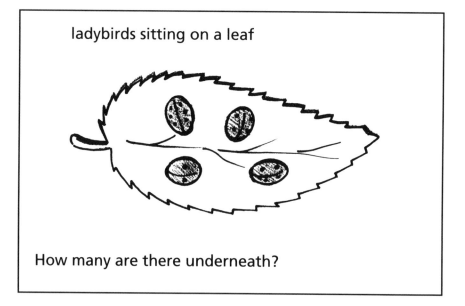

ladybirds sitting on a leaf

How many are there underneath?

Design for Rosie the hen

Make Rosie the hen from fabric or card, with two 'working' wings under which she can keep her chicks. A Velcro strip secures each felt chick under the wing.

Photocopiable sheet for calculator numbers

Sorting diagrams

This page provides information about different types of sorting diagram for use with logic activities.

Carroll diagram

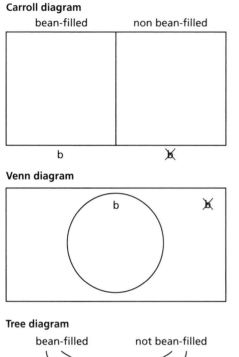

Carroll diagram

Children:	wearing a watch	not wearing a watch	
wearing a belt	Sanjay	Catherine	b
not wearing a belt	Gareth	Alex	X̶
	w	X̶	

Venn diagram

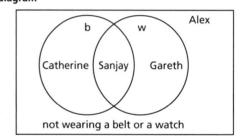

not wearing a belt or a watch

Tree diagram

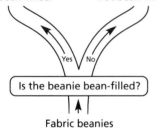

Tree diagram

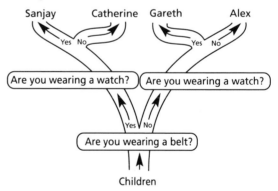

Fabric beanies – how to make a set

Make a set of fabric beanies. (Better still, ask parents to make the set.) Cut circles of material the size of a teaplate. Add felt mouths and eyes, keeping features as similar as possible. Fill six beanies with dried beans and fill six with kapok.

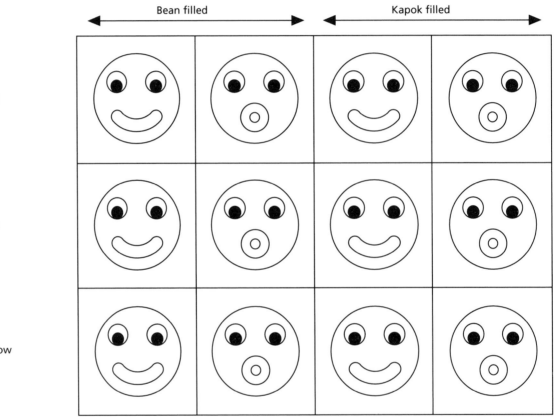

Resources

Blank playing cards	AMS Educational
0–100 cards	AMS Educational
Blank dice	Hope Catalogue
Compare Bears	GLS Catalogue
Construct-o-straws	Hope Catalogue
'Count me in' games	AMS Educational
Cuisenaire	NES/Arnold Catalogue
Dienes M.A.B.	NES/Arnold Catalogue
Foam Dice	Hope Catalogue
Logic Blocks	NES/Arnold Catalogue
Logic People	Hope Catalogue
Multilingual number stickers	AMS Educational
Multilink	NES/Arnold Catalogue
Nine-spot dominoes	NES/Arnold Catalogue
Numbers in place mats	AMS Educational
Number lines	AMS Educational
OHP calculator TI 106	Oxford Educational Supplies Ltd
Pegboards	GLS Catalogue
Pip	Swallow Systems
Pixie	
Polydron	Hope Catalogue
Roamer	Valiant Technology Ltd
Sand and Water Resources Pack	NES/Arnold Catalogue
SMILE: the First 31	Smile Centre
SLIMWAM	Association of Teachers of Mathematics
Tiling generators	Association of Teachers of Mathematics
Unifix	GLS Catalogue
Unifix underlays	GLS Catalogue
What's in the Square?	GLS Catalogue

Addresses

AMS Educational
Woodside Trading Estate
Low Lane
Horsforth
Leeds
LS18 5NY
Tel: 0113 258 0309
Fax: 0113 258 0133

Association of Teachers of Mathematics
7 Shaftesbury St
Derby
DE23 8YB
Tel: 01332 356599
Fax: 01332 204357

GLS
Fairway
1 Mollison Avenue
Enfield
EN3 7XQ
Tel: 0181 805 8333

Hope Catalogue
Orb Mill
Huddersfield Rd
Oldham
OL4 2ST
Tel: 0161 633 6611

NES/Arnold
Ludlow Hill Rd
West Bridgford
Nottingham
NG2 6HD
Tel: 0115 971 7717
Fax: 0500 410420

Oxford Educational Supplies Ltd
Unit 19
Weston Business Park
Weston on the Green
Bicester
Oxon
OX6 8SY
Tel: 01869 343369
Fax: 01869 343654

SMILE Centre
108A Lancaster Rd
London
W11 1QS
Tel: 0171 221 8966

Swallow Systems
32 High St
High Wycombe
Bucks
HP11 2AQ
Tel: 0494 813471

Valiant Technology Ltd
Gulf House
370 Old York Rd
Wandsworth
London
SW18 1SP
Tel: 0181 874 8747

Bibliography

Baratta Lorton, M. (1976) *Mathematics Their Way*. London: Addison Wesley.

Baratta Lorton, M. (1979) *Workjobs 2*. London: Addison Wesley.

Bird, M.H. (1991) *Mathematics for Young Children*. London: Routledge.

Cobb, P. (1986) Context, goals, beliefs and learning mathematics, *For the Learning of Mathematics*, 6(2), 2–9.

Denvir, B. and Brown, M. (1986) Understanding of number concepts in low attaining 7–9 year olds, *Educational Studies in Mathematics*, 17, 15–36 and 143–64.

Donaldson, M. (1978) *Children's Minds*. London: Fontana.

Fielker, D. (1993a) *Starting from Your Head: Mental Number*. London: The BEAM Project.

Fielker, D. (1993b) *Starting from Your Head: Mental Geometry*. London: The BEAM Project.

Gifford, S., Mosley, F., Ebbutt, S. and Barber, P. (1992) *Starting from Number Lines*. London: The BEAM Project.

Hughes, M. (1986) *Children and Number*. Oxford: Basil Blackwell.

ILEA (1985) *Count Me In*. London: ILEA.

Lerman, S. (1989) Investigations: where to now?, in P. Ernest (ed.) *Mathematics Teaching: the State of the Art*. Falmer: Lewes.

Pound, L., Cook, L., Court, J., Stevenson, J. and Wadsworth, J. (1992) *The Early Years: Mathematics*. London: Harcourt, Brace, Jovanovich.

Skemp, R.R. (1989) *Mathematics in the Primary School*. London: Routledge.

Thompson, I. (1995) Pre number activities and the early years number curriculum, *Mathematics in School*, 24(1), 37–9.

Vygotsky, L.S. (1978) *Mind in Society: the Development of the Higher Psychological Processes*. London: Harvard University Press.

THE EXCELLENCE OF PLAY

Janet R. Moyles (ed.)

Child: When I play with my friends we have lots of fun . . . do lots
of things . . . think about stuff . . . and . . . well . . .
Adult: Do you think you learn anything?
Child: Heaps and heaps – not like about sums and books and
things . . . um . . . like . . . well . . . like *real* things.

Anyone who has observed play for any length of time will recognize that, for young children, play is a tool for learning. Professionals who understand, acknowledge, and appreciate this can, through provision, interaction and intervention in children's play, ensure progression, differentiation and relevance in the curriculum.

The Excellence of Play gathers together authoritative contributors to provide a wide-ranging and key source text reflecting both up-to-date research and current classroom practice. It tackles how we conceptualize play, how we 'place' it in the classroom, how we relate it to the curriculum, and how we evaluate its role in learning in the early years. It will stimulate and inform debate through its powerful argument that 'a curriculum which sanctions and utilizes play is more likely to provide well-balanced citizens of the future as well as happier children in the present.

Contents

Contributors

Lesley Abbott, Angela Anning, Tony Bertram, David Brown, Tina Bruce, Audrey Curtis, Rose Griffiths, Nigel Hall, Peter Heaslip, Jane Hislam, Victoria Hurst, Neil Kitson, Janet R. Moyles, Christine Pascal, Roy Prentice, Jeni Riley, Jane Savage, Peter K. Smith.

240pp   0 335 19068 5 (Paperback)